故園畫憶

庚寅中秋
韓馨渔題

《故园画忆系列》编委会

名誉主任： 韩启德

主　　任： 邵　鸿

委　　员：（按姓氏笔画为序）

万　捷	王秋桂	方李莉	叶培贵
刘魁立	况　晗	严绍璗	吴为山
范贻光	范　芳	孟　白	邵　鸿
岳庆平	郑培凯	唐晓峰	曹兵武

故园画忆系列
Memory of the Old
Home in Sketches

豫东印象
Impression of Eastern Henan Province

王金志　绘画　撰文
Sketches & Notes by Wang Jinzhi

学苑出版社
Academy Press

图书在版编目（CIP）数据

豫东印象 / 王金志绘画、撰文. -- 北京：学苑出版社，2015.10
（故园画忆系列）
ISBN 978-7-5077-4886-4

Ⅰ.①豫… Ⅱ.①王… Ⅲ.①钢笔画—作品集—中国—现代②河南省—概况 Ⅳ.①J224②K926.1

中国版本图书馆CIP数据核字（2015）第242263号

出 版 人：	孟　白
责 任 编 辑：	周　鼎
出版发行：	学苑出版社
社　　　址：	北京市丰台区南方庄2号院1号楼
邮 政 编 码：	100079
网　　　址：	www.book001.com
电 子 信 箱：	xueyuanpress@163.com
联 系 电 话：	010-67601101（营销部）、67603091（总编室）
经　　　销：	全国新华书店
印 刷 厂：	三河市灵山红旗印刷厂
开 本 尺 寸：	889×1194　1/24
印　　　张：	6.25
字　　　数：	146千字
图　　　幅：	128幅
版　　　次：	2015年11月北京第1版
印　　　次：	2015年11月北京第1次印刷
定　　　价：	45.00元

目 录

自 序　　　　　　　　　王金志

商丘市

燧皇陵	3
火神台	4
仓颉墓	5
伊尹墓	6
微子墓	7
三陵台	8
葵丘会盟台	9
承匡城遗址	10
庄周墓	11
芒砀山汉墓群	12
江淹墓	13
隋唐大运河码头遗址	14
黄河故道	15
商丘古城墙	16
归德府文庙	17
永城文庙	18
孔子还乡祠	19
花木兰祠	20
张巡祠	21
汤文正公祠	22
李氏家祠	23
吕祖庙	24
白云寺	25
崇法寺塔	26
圣寿寺塔	27
无忧寺塔	28
双状元塔	29
八关斋会报德记碑亭	30
侯府	31
壮悔堂	32
穆氏四合院	33
睢县东关清真寺	34
宁陵清真寺	35
商丘天主教堂	36
圣保罗医院	37
毛泽东视察黄楼纪念馆	38
中共中原局扩大会议旧址	39
中共中央中原局扩大会议秘书处旧址	40
陈官庄淮海战役纪念馆	41
彭雪枫纪念馆	42
夏邑二鬼摔跤	43
李秀山泥塑	44
夏邑县火店镇灯笼村	45
永城市茴村镇书法村	46
民权县农民画	47
火神台庙会	48
四平调	49

麒麟舞 50

开封市

开封城墙 53
龙亭 54
开封府文庙 55
铁塔 56
相国寺 57
繁塔 58
延庆观 59
太平兴国寺 60
杞县大云寺塔 61
开封东大寺 62
北清真寺 63
朱仙镇岳飞庙 64
山陕甘会馆 65
孟子游梁祠 66
无梁庙 67
禹王台 68
镇河铁犀 69
河南贡院 70
河南大学·博雅楼 71
河南大学·大礼堂 72
本笃修女会会堂 73
朱仙镇清真寺 74
开封市天主教堂 75
天主教河南总修道院 76
陈留天主教堂 77

禹王台红楼 78
国共"黄河归故"谈判旧址 79
兴隆火车站旧址 80
刘青霞故居 81
华北体育场旧址 82
刘少奇在开封陈列馆 83
田家宅院 84
开封盘鼓 85
开封风筝 86
大相国寺梵乐 87
朱仙镇木版年画 88
汴京灯笼张 89
通许锣戏 90
开封斗鸡 91
汴绣 92
开封二夹弦 93
撂石锁 94

周口市

昆山女娲宫 97
西华县女娲城 98
南顿故城 99
太清宫 100
老君台 101
太昊陵 102
画卦台 103
弦歌台 104
端敏袁公祠 105

关帝庙	106	吉鸿昌将军纪念馆	121
太康文庙	107	逍遥镇水闸	122
扶沟大程书院	108	周口公园	123
西华县明伦堂	109	周口市博物馆	124
西华县城隍庙	110	西华胡辣汤	125
太康小吴塔	111	扶沟县烟雾山庙会	126
太康寿圣寺塔	112	周口越调	127
商水寿圣寺塔	113	太昊陵庙会	128
西华县龙泉寺	114	官会锣鼓	129
千年古刹支亭寺	115	祭拜伏羲大典	130
陈州街清真寺	116	太康道情戏	131
淮阳城关镇清真大寺	117	淮阳县泥泥狗	132
叶氏庄园	118	周口渔鼓	133
袁世凯故居	119	沈丘回族文狮舞	134
袁世凯行宫（项城博物馆）	120		

Contents

Preface   Wang Jinzhi

Shangqiu City

Imperial Sui Mausoleum	3
Stand of God of Fire	4
Cang Jie Tomb	5
Yi Yin Tomb	6
Wei Zi Tomb	7
Three-Mausoleum Platform	8
Kuiqiu Alliance Temple	9
Chengkuangcheng Ruins	10
Zhuang Zhou Tomb	11
Mangdang Mountain Tombs, Western Han Dynasty	12
Jiang Yan Tomb	13
Sui and Tang Dynasty Wharf Ruins of the Grand Canal	14
National Forest Park of the Yellow River Old Course	15
Shangqiu Ancient City Wall	16
Guidefu Confucian Temple	17
Yongcheng Mangshan Confucian Temple	18
Confucius Temple	19
Hua Mulan Temple	20
Zhang Xun Shrine	21
Tang Wenzhenggong Shrine	22
Lee Clan Ancestral Hall	23
Lü Zu Temple	24
Minquan Baiyun Temple	25
Yongcheng Chongfa Temple Pagoda	26
Shengshou Temple Pagoda	27
Wuyou Temple Pagoda	28
Dual-Champion Pagodas of Minquan County	29
Eight Precepts Association Moral Report Pavilion	30
Hou Mansion	31
Hall of Remorse for Youth	32
Mu Clan Quadrangle Courtyard	33
Dongguan Mosque of Suixian County	34
Yuan Dynasty Ningling Mosque	35
Shangqiu Catholic Church	36
St. Paul Hospital	37
Mao Zedong Memorial Hall	38
Expanded Meeting Site of the Central Plains Bureau of the Central Committee	39
Secretariat of the Expanded Meeting Site of the Central Plains Bureau of the Central Committee	40
Chenguanzhuang Huaihai Campaign Memorial	41
Peng Xuefeng Memorial	42
Two Ghosts Wrestling of Xiayi	43

Clay Sculpture of Li Xiushan	44	Zhuxian Town Mosque	74
Lantern Village, Huodian Town Xiayi County	45	Catholic Church of Kaifeng	75
Calligraphy Village in Huicun Town, Yongcheng	46	Henan Catholic Monastery	76
		Chenliu Catholic Church	77
Farmers' Paintings of Minquan County	47	Yuwang Platform "Red Building"	78
Temple Fair in Stand of God of Fire	48	Nationalist and Communist Negotiation Site	79
Siping Tune	49	Xinglong Railway Station	80
Unicorn Dance	50	Liu Qingxia's Former Residence	81
		North China Stadium Site	82

Kaifeng City

		Liu Shaoqi Exhibition Hall in Kaifeng	83
Kaifeng City Walls	53	Tian Clan Residence	84
Dragon Pavilion	54	Kaifeng Drum	85
Kaifeng Confucius Temple	55	Kiafeng Kites	86
Iron Tower	56	Buddhist Music at Daxiangguo Temple	87
Xiangguo Temple	57	Woodblock New Year Painting Clubs, Zhuxian Town	88
Fan Tower	58		
Yanqing Taoist Temple	59	Bianjing Lantern Zhang Family	89
Taiping Xingguo Temple	60	Tongxu Gong Play	90
Dayun Temple Tower, Qixian County	61	Kaifeng Cockfights	91
Kaifeng East Temple	62	Bian Embroidery	92
North Mosque	63	Two-clip String of Kaifeng	93
Yuefei Temple, Zhuxian Town	64	Knock Lock	94
Shanxi-Shaanxi-Gansu Guild Hall	65		

Zhoukou City

Mencius Temple	66	Kunshan Nüwa Palace	97
Wuliang Temple	67	Nüwa Town, Xihua County	98
Yuwang Platform	68	Nandun Ancient City	99
River-Guarding Iron Rhinoceros	69	Taiqing Palace	100
Henan Examination Hall	70	Laojun Platform	101
Henan University (1)	71	Taihao Mausoleum	102
Henan University (2)	72	Eight Diagrams Platform	103
Bendu Sisters Hall	73		

Xiange Platform	104	General Ji Hongchang Memorial Hall	121
Upright Duke Yuan's Temple	105	Water Gate of Xiaoyao Town	122
Guanyu Temple	106	Zhoukou Park	123
Confucius Temple of Taikang	107	Zhoukou City Museum	124
Fugou Dacheng Academy	108	Xihua Pepper Soup	125
Minglun Hall, Xihua County	109	Temple Fair of Yanwu Mountain Fugou County	126
Chenghuang Temple of Xihua County	110		
Xiaowu Pagoda of Taikang County	111	Yue Opera of Zhoukou	127
Shousheng Temple Pagoda in Taikang	112	Taihao Mausoleum Temple Fair in Huaiyang Zhoukou	128
Pagoda of Shousheng Temple in Shangshui	113		
Longquan Temple of Xihua County	114	Guanhui Gongs and Drums	129
Zhiting Ancient Temple	115	Worship Ceremony of Fu Xi in Huaiyang Zhoukou	130
Chenzhou Street Mosque	116		
Mosque of Chengguan Town Huaiyang	117	Taikang Daoqing Opera (Rhyme of Taoist)	131
Ye Family Manor	118	Huaiyang County Clay Dog	132
Former Residence of Yuan Shikai	119	Zhoukou Bamboo Drum	133
Temporary Imperial Palace of Yuan Shikai (Xiangcheng Museum)	120	Shenqiu Hui People's Lion Dance	134

自 序

  《豫东印象》以"豫东地区"的历史名胜古迹和非物质文化遗产为对象,以速写的方式记录当下的,也是历史的一个瞬间,并辅以简要文字说明,共128幅画作。

  "豫东地区"指河南省东部的商丘、开封、周口三个省辖市及其市县的行政区域,与鲁、苏、皖三省接壤,在这片黄淮大平原上孕育了黄河文明,是中华文明的发祥地之一。

  商丘,系国家历史文化名城,"商丘"二字源自轩辕氏黄帝的四世孙阏伯,阏伯是帝喾高辛氏的儿子,曾经辅佐大禹治水,因功受封于商,被赐为"子"姓。"商"在骨文中为"禸",上为"子",下为"冈",意为"子"姓的人生活在高岗上。古时此地多丘岭,人们为了逃避洪水,多生活在高丘上。古时人们把居住地或坟墓称为"丘",阏伯死后又葬此地"冈"上、亦"丘",为纪念阏伯,故名"商丘"。现存阏伯台,是帝尧时期的古观星台遗址,是我国最古老的天文台遗址,距今约有4500年的历史。商丘是中华文明的发祥地之一,商丘的历史同中华5000年的文明史同步,燧人氏在这里发明了人工取火,结束了人类茹毛饮血的历史。商丘是商部族的起源和聚居地,商人、商业、商文化的发源地,商朝开国帝王商汤灭夏后最早建都地,史称"三商之源"。商丘人文历史景观星罗棋布:商丘古城、宋国故城、应天书院、燧皇陵、隋唐大运河遗址、归德府文庙、梁园遗址、张巡祠、八关斋、庄周墓、微子祠等古迹众多。

  开封,简称汴,古称老丘、大梁、汴梁、东京、汴京,中国七大古都之一,国家级历史文化名城,中原经济区的核心城市。历史上曾先后有夏、魏、后梁、后晋、后汉、后周、北宋、金朝八个朝代在此建都,被誉为"八朝古都"。尤其在北宋时期,东京(开封)是全国政治、经济、文化的中心,中国古代历史上经济与文化教育最繁荣的时代,也是当时世界上最繁华的大都市之一。明朝开封为周王府所在地,中原第一都会。自清朝至新中国成立初期,开封一直是河南的政治、经济、文化中心。开封文化底蕴深厚、文物古迹众多,如开封古城墙、开封铁塔、龙亭、大相国寺、山陕甘会馆、禹王台、包公祠、开封府、朱仙镇、岳飞庙、河南大学近现代建筑群、清明上河园、宋都御街、书店街等。

  周口,地属黄淮平原腹地,原是沙颍河上的重要的货运码头,可入淮河、汇长江,直达南京、上海。周口是伏羲故都,老子故里,为中华文化发祥的重地。淮阳是"太昊伏羲氏都",平粮台是距今4000多年前的龙山文化遗址,也是我国目前发现最早的古城之一。周口鹿邑是老子故里、道家发源地、陈抟老祖故里,关于老子与道家遗迹颇丰。项城市有南顿故城、袁氏故居。

  我在长期的资料整理、采风写生的过程中,常常为豫东厚重的历史文化遗迹而自豪不已,也会因一些历史文化遗迹的消失而深感惋惜,尤其是为一些未能列入文物保护范围的古建筑的命运堪忧。希望通过此书的出版,能唤起更多人对历史文化遗产的重视。

民间民俗文化是民族精神的重要载体,是民族文化的主要组成部分。中原地区民俗具有典型的华夏文明之"根"的特征,豫东民间民俗又深刻代表了中国农耕文化的特征。书中所涉及的民俗部分只是豫东丰富多彩民俗文化的一点一滴,以速写的形式表现,远不能道出豫东民俗特点的真正内涵。

我想对于星罗棋布的现存的文物及人文景观而言,又何尝不是如此呢,难免会挂一漏万。艺海无涯,望各位同仁批评指正。

是以为序,与读者共飨。

王金志

2014 年 12 月 8 日

Preface

Impression of Eastern Henan Province, which contains 120 drawings of places of historic interest and intangible cultural heritage, records the present moment and a moment in history by means of sketches and brief captions.

"Eastern Henan" refers to the administrative areas of Shangqiu, Kaifeng and Zhoukou, which are the three provincial-level cities in the east part of Henan Province, and their subsidiary counties. The Huanghuai Plain, where eastern Henan is situated, has bred the Yellow River civilization and is one of the birthplaces of Chinese national culture.

Shangqiu, the ancient capital city of six dynasties, has a history synchronized with China's 5,000-year civilization. The mastery of fire starting by Suirenshi here ended the primitive human barbarism history. This ancient city is the origin of the Shang Tribe and the birthplace of merchant, commerce and business culture.

Kaifeng, also called Bian, is an ancient capital of eight dynasties and a core city in the Central Plains Economic Zone. During the Northern Song Dynasty (960-1127), in particular, Dongjing (Kaifeng) was China's political, economic and cultural center and one of the world's most flourishing cities at the time.

Zhoukou, located in the heart of the Huanghuai Plain, was originally an important port on the Shaying River. Waters from here flow through the Huaihe River, the Yangtze River past Nanjing and enter the ocean at Shanghai. Zhoukou is the hometown of Fuxi and Lao-tzu, making it an important birthplace of the Chinese culture.

Having dedicated much time to compiling data, investigating customs and sketching, I am deeply proud of the profound historical and cultural relics in eastern Henan Province. Meanwhile, I deeply regret the disappearance of some historical and cultural relics and feel that the fate of some ancient structures, which have not been included in the cultural relic protection scope, is worrying. I hope that the publication of this book will attract more people's attention to historical and cultural heritage.

Folk culture is an important carrier of national spirit and a major part of the national culture. The folklore of the Central Plains is a source of Chinese civilization. The folk culture of eastern Henan Province, in particular, represents the characteristics of overall Chinese culture. The folklore presented in this book is just a very small part of the rich and colorful folk culture of the eastern Henan Province. Presented in the form of sketches, it is far from the full meaning of the folk characteristics of the region. Since there are no boundaries in the arts, I look forward to comments, criticism and corrections from my colleagues.

That's why I wrote this preface to share my opinions with readers.

Wang Jinzhi
December 8th, 2014

商丘市
Shangqiu City

燧皇陵

又称燧人氏陵，位于商丘市西南的阏伯台村。燧人氏，传说中的钻木取火者。墓冢前原有一石碑，上刻"燧人氏陵"，今碑毁不存。皇陵现已扩建，占地30万平方米左右，燧人氏墓冢和雕像矗立于陵区的中心。墓冢呈方锥型，长、宽均为82米，高13.9米，前面延伸有神道，两侧有龙凤麒麟等石像，周围有松柏环绕。

Imperial Sui Mausoleum

Situated at Quebotai Village in southwest Shangqiu, it is also called Suirenshi Mausoleum. Suirenshi was the legendary discoverer of fire using the wood drilling method. The pyramid-shaped tomb, surrounded by lush cypresses, is 82 meters in width and length and 13.9 meters high.

| 火神台 |

位于商丘市火星台村，又名阙伯台、火星台。传帝喾封子阙伯为"火正"，于商丘主辰星之祀，卒后商丘人筑台葬之，因称阙伯台。始建于元大德年间（1297～1307年），明清重修。台高35米，周长270米，夯筑而成。台上有禅门、大殿、配殿和拜殿。大殿面阔三间，进深三间，硬山琉璃瓦间灰瓦顶，殿内有壁画。

Stand of God of Fire

Located at Huoxingtai Village in Shangqiu, the Stand of the Fire God of Fire is also known as Quebo Stand and Huoxing Stand. Some legends say Emperor Ku made his son Quebo the minister was responsible for star worship. The Stand of the God of Fire, with a history of more than 700 years, 35 meters high with a perimeter of 270 meters, consists of a Gate to Buddhism, a main hall, a side hall and an altar.

仓颉墓

　　位于虞城县王集乡堌堆坡村西。仓颉是我国传说中的文字创始者,为斯文开天之祖。现存墓冢高三米,周长 31 米,原有汉熹平六年(177 年)立仓颉墓碑,已无存。现前立石碑一通,阴刻"古仓颉墓"四字。墓前存清康熙九年(1670 年)重修仓颉祠大殿三间及东西配房,殿前古柏两株。

Cang Jie Tomb

The tomb is located west of Guduipo, at Wangji Village, Yucheng County. According to legend, Cang Jie invented Chinese writing. The tomb is 3meters high with a 31-meter circumference. The main hall, Cang Jie Temple Hall rebuilt in 1670, has two ancient cypresses in front.

伊尹墓

　　位于商丘市虞城县站集乡魏堌堆村。伊尹为商初大臣，又名挚。传出身奴隶，后辅佐汤灭夏，历辅外丙、中壬，逐太甲，沃丁时死，葬于亳。现冢高三米，面积约60平方米，四周广植松柏。原冢前有伊尹祠，已废。现已修复花戏楼，另有历代祭祀碑碣20余通。

Yi Yin Tomb

This tomb of Yi Yin is situated in Weigudui Village, Zhanji Township, Yucheng County, Shangqiu. Yi Yin was a minister at the beginning of the Shang Dynasty (17th-11th Century BC). Born as a slave, legends holds, Yi Yin helped Emperor Tang of the Shang Dynasty annihilate the Xia Dynasty (21st-17th Century BC). The 3-meter high tomb is surrounded by cypresses.

微子墓

位于睢阳区路河乡青岗寺集，为商纣王庶兄微子（名启）之墓。周公诛武庚封微子于宋，以继殷祀，卒后葬于此。现墓冢被平，墓前尚存明万历四十一年（1613年）归德府知府郑三俊立碑一通，上刻"殷微子之墓"。墓上原建祭祀庙宇不存。

Wei Zi Tomb

Wei Zi was the younger brother of Emperor Zhou of the Shang Dynasty (1765-1122). The tomb is located west of Qinggangsi Village of Luhe, Suiyang District. A 1613 inscription tablet stands in the front of the tomb.

三陵台

周成王三年（前1039年），微子启封宋国，都睢阳（今商丘），历26世、34君。戴公于周宣王二十九年（前799年）即位，在位34年，传位其子武公司空，18年后，武公传位其子宣公。戴、武、宣三公祖孙均葬于此，因三陵并峙，故名三陵台。图为宋戴公陵。

Three-Mausoleum Platform

According to historical records, Wei Zi was granted land in Sui-yang (now Shangqiu), where the Song capital was built. His descendants, Dukes Dai, Wu and Xuan are all buried here in three adjacent tombs, thus it is called Three-Mausoleum Platform. The sketch shows the Tomb of Duke Song.

葵丘会盟台

位于民权县林的黄河故道北岸，是周襄王元年（前651年）齐桓公会盟诸侯之地。春秋时期，周平王东迁，王室地位和权威削弱，诸侯纷争，齐桓公在管仲相助下，重农商、轻赋税，壮大经济，国力强盛。为了进一步巩固自己的权威，其在位43年，会盟诸侯达26次。葵丘会盟对当时的经济发展、社会稳定具有重要意义。

Kuiqiu Alliance Temple

Located on the north shore of an old course of the Yellow River in Minquan County, Kuiqiu Alliance Temple is where Duke Huan of Qi met kings of neighboring states to form alliances in the year 651 BC. Duke Huan was one of the five governors of the Spring and Autumn Period (722-418). Alliance was of great significance for economic development and social stability at that time.

承匡城遗址

　　位于睢县县城西匡城村。承匡城是春秋时宋之城邑，周朝秦康公，假借刚即位的周匡之名在匡地筑城，后还宋，名承匡城，至今已有 2600 余年的历史。该城约 7.5 平方千米，现保存有部分城墙。

Chengkuangcheng Ruins

A Song state site of the Spring and Autumn Period, Chengkuangcheng's history can be traced back than 2,600 years. Located at Xikuangcheng Village in Suixian County, the ruins cover an area of about 7.5 square kilometers; some city walls remain.

庄周墓

位于民权县老颜集乡唐庄村东,庄周(约前369~前286年)宋国蒙(今民权县清莲寺村)人,战国杰出思想家,道家学派的重要创始人之一。现存墓冢高两米,呈圆锥形,面积约20平方米。墓前有清乾隆年间(1736~1795年)立墓碑一通,碑阳刻"庄周之墓",碑阴刻"重修庄周墓碑记题名"。

Zhuang Zhou Tomb

The tomb is east of Tangzhuang Village of Laoyanji, Minquan County. Zhuang Zhou (circa 369- 286), born in the state of Song, was an outstanding thinker and one of the crucial founders of Taoism. The conical-shaped tomb is two meters high.

芒砀山汉墓群

　　位于永城市芒砀山，为西汉梁国王陵，包括梁孝王陵、梁孝王王后陵、梁共王陵、僖山墓等。墓群分布在除芒砀山主峰之外的各个山峰上，已发掘21座，范围约550多万平方米。墓群斩山作廓，穿石为藏，结构复杂，气势恢宏，宛如庞大的地下宫殿。

Mangdang Mountain Tombs, Western Han Dynasty

Located at Mangdang Mountain in Yongcheng, they are the imperial mausoleums of the Liang state in the Western Han Dynasty. 21 tombs covering an area of about 5.5 million square meters have been excavated. They are spectacular, like huge underground palaces.

江淹墓

位于民权县李堂乡岳庄村西。江淹（444～505年），考城（今民权县江集村）人，南北朝时文学家、政治家，一生历宋、齐、梁三代。墓冢高2.3米，面积约25平方米，前有明成化年间（1465～1487年）立的墓碑一通，上书"齐醴陵侯金紫光禄大夫江文通之墓"，保存完好。

Jiang Yan Tomb

Situated west of Yuezhuang Village of Litang, Minquan County, the well-preserved 2.3-meter high tomb dates from the Ming Dynasty (1368–1644). Jiang Yan (444-505) was a literary figure and politician of the Northern and Southern Dynasties (420-589).

隋唐大运河码头遗址

　　位于商丘市睢阳区商柘公路与105国道之间,北岸占地约24.5万平方米,南岸占地约24.8万平方米。商丘市大运河是隋唐时期京杭大运河通济渠的重要组成部分,夏邑县汴河济阳镇段至今仍保存有宽20～30米、长20多千米的运河水面。

Sui and Tang Dynasty Wharf Ruins of the Grand Canal

Located at Suiyang District in Shangqiu, it covers an area of about 250,000 square meters. The section of the Grand Canal within Shangqiu was an important part of the Tongji Channel of the Beijing-Hangzhou Grand Canal during the Sui (581-618) and Tang (618-907) dynasties. Jiyang Town section of the Bian River in Xiayi County still remains; canal waters are 20-30 meters wide and over 20 kilometers long.

| 黄河故道 |

位于商丘市北部。明万历年间（1573～1620年）工部尚书潘季驯，采用"束水攻沙以水治水"方略，动用了五万民工历时16年，修筑了南北两条大堤，结束了400年的黄河之灾，清末黄河改道而成故堤。保存完好，长134千米，高10～13米。

National Forest Park of the Yellow River Old Course

National Forest Park is alongside the old Yellow River course, in northern Shangqiu. During Ming Emperor Wanli's reign (1573-1620), governors built two levees here, ending a 400-year danger of devastating Yellow River floods. The two levees 134 kilometers long and 10-13 meters high are well preserved.

商丘古城墙

又称归德府城墙，位于商丘市睢阳区，建于明正德六年（1511年）。呈南北长方形，砖砌，周长4355米，高6.6米，底宽10米，顶宽七米，有3600个垛口，四角均设有突出城外的角台。城有四券门，城内120多条街，每街长200米，纵横交错，整齐划一。城外有护城河及护城大堤。保存基本完好。

Shangqiu Ancient City Wall

Also called Guidefu City Wall, located at Suiyang District in Shangqiu, this brick city wall was built in 1511 in a south-north rectangle with a perimeter of 4,355 meters and at a height of 6.60 meters. The ancient city has four gates and more than 120 streets, each 200 meters long, neatly crisscrossing the city. Outside the city, moats and levees protect the city.

归德府文庙

位于商丘县城中山北三街，始建于元延佑四年（1317年），明洪武六年（1373年）、正德年间（1505～1521年）、清乾隆年间（1736～1795年）增建重修。现存大成殿一座，面阔七间，进深三间，歇山式琉璃瓦顶，有脊饰；明伦堂一座，面阔五间，进深三间，歇山式瓦顶，有脊饰。明、清重修碑记五通。

Guidefu Confucian Temple

On Zhongshan North Third Street in Shangqiu, the temple was built in 1317. Dacheng Hall with glazed-tile roof and ridge decorations is well preserved. Minglun Hall has a gable and hip tile roof. Five steles repaired in the Ming (1368-1644) and Qing (1644-1911) dynasties remain.

商丘归德府文庙

永城文庙

　　位于永城县芒山镇夫子山南麓，始建年代不详，现存为清末建筑。现有山门三间，硬山灰瓦顶；启圣殿一座，面阔五间，进深三间，歇山灰瓦顶，下有砖、石台基；东西厢房各三间，硬山灰瓦顶，保存较好。庙内还有清代、民国年间碑刻三通，古柏多株。

Yongcheng Mangshan Confucian Temple

At the southern foot of Fuzi Mountain in Mangshan Town, Yongcheng County, the temple has no known construction date. The existing structure was built in the late Qing Dynasty (1644-1911). The monastery gate, Qisheng Hall and east-west wing rooms are better preserved. There are three inscriptions of the Qing Dynasty and the Republic of China (1912-1949) and several ancient cypresses.

孔子还乡祠

位于夏邑县城北王公楼村,此地为春秋时期宋国,孔子祖居所在地。周僖王二年(前 680 年),宋国发生内乱,孔子曾祖为避乱而奔鲁国,孔子成人后时常回祖籍祭祖省亲。祠堂始建于唐初,其形制仿文庙,坐北朝南,有一壁、一坛、两殿、四门及碑林等。宋代曾修复扩建,金代在大成殿前立杏坛碑,清道光元年(1821 年)增建崇圣祠。

Confucius Temple

The Temple was built at Wanggonglou Village of Chengbei, Xiayi County, the ancestral homeland of Confucius who lived in the Song State of the Spring and Autumn Period. He often came back to his ancestral homeland to worship his ancestors. Built at the beginning of the Tang Dynasty, the temple faces south and has an altar, two halls, and steles.

花木兰祠

位于虞城县营廓镇，为纪念巾帼英雄花木兰而兴建。花木兰在唐初被追封为"孝烈将军"并为其修建此祠堂，占地面积一万多平方米。元泰和年间（1201～1206年）、元统二年（1334年）大修，立有《孝烈将军祠像辨证记》石碑一通。清嘉庆十一年（1806年）春，再次大修，立《孝烈将军祠辨误正名记》石碑一通。

Hua Mulan Temple

The temple, situated at Yingguo Town, Yucheng County, was built in memory of female heroine Hua Mulan. Temple construction began during the Tang Dynasty and underwent repairs during the Yuan (1280-1368) and Qing Dynasty (1644-1911). Of the stone steles erected, only two remain.

张巡祠

即六忠祠，又名忠烈祠，位于商丘古城中山西二街。始建于唐至德二年（757年），为纪念"安史之乱"睢阳守卫战中张巡等人而建，并以其部将南霁云配享，称协忠庙，后增雷万春、贾贲、姚訚配享，改称六忠祠。现存过厅二间，均为硬山灰瓦顶，有脊饰，大门和厢房已改建。祠内存有明天启四年（1572年）所立碑刻一通。

Zhang Xun Shrine

Also known as Liuzhong Shrine and National Heroes Shrine, it is located on Zhongshan West Second Street in Shangqiu. It was built in 757 in memory of Zhang Xun and other soldiers who died guarding Suiyang District during the Tang Dynasty Anshi Rebellion. The entrance door and wing rooms have been rebuilt.

| 汤文正公祠 |

又名汤文正公贤良祠,位于睢县县城西大街路北。汤斌(1627～1687年),清朝大儒,理学名臣,清代重臣之首,被誉为"三代帝王师、天下文官祖",参与编修《明史》《大清会典》等及历任要职。汤斌去世后,朝廷赐谥号"文正公"。今仅存头门及祠内大殿六间。

Tang Wenzhenggong Shrine
Situated of Xidajie Road in Suixian County, the shrine is for the incorruptible official Tang Bin of the Qing Dynasty. Tang Bin, (1627 -1687), was an important official holding key positions. Only the entrance door and six main halls remain.

李氏家祠

位于商丘市梁园区孙福集乡乔楼村，曾为乔楼小学。面阔三间，看似三层，实为两层，上部为装饰。建筑风格厚重古朴，装饰雕刻精美，上部正中镶有"李氏先祠"四个大字，门脸上刻有"木本水源"，祠堂前面松柏掩映，肃穆庄严。

Lee Clan Ancestral Hall

Located at Qiaolou Village of Sunfuji Town in Liangyuan District, Shangqiu, the hall used to be the Qiaolou Primary School. The architecture style is of primitive simplicity and cultural significance. The decorations are beautifully carved. In the middle of the upper part are four inlaid Chinese characters meaning Li Clan Ancestral Hall.

吕祖庙

位于睢县城关镇东南隅,俗称袁家山,为明代天启年间(1621～1627年)尚书袁可立祭祀吕洞宾而建。清代重修,坐北朝南。建在高七米的土台上。有山门一间,硬山灰瓦顶;大殿一座,面阔三间,进深三间,硬山卷棚勾连搭琉璃瓦、灰瓦顶;大殿后有吕祖洞、八仙亭。现存清咸丰年间(1851～1861年)和光绪二十九年(1903年)碑刻一通。保存较好。

Lü Zu Temple

Located at the southeast corner of Chengguan Town, Suixian County, Lü Zu Temple, also called Yuanjia Mountain Temple, was built by Yuan Keli, a minister during Ming Tianqi's reign period (1621-1627) to worship immortal Lv Dongbin. The south-facing temple has a monastery gate, main hall, Lü Zu hole and Eight-Immortal Pavilion.

> 白云寺

　　原为白衣庵，位于民权县尹店乡白云寺村。建于唐贞观年间（627～649年），坐北朝南，明清重修和扩建。现存韦驮殿、罗汉殿、大雄宝殿、禅堂各一座及东西厢房各五间，寺内外有石经幢、铁钟、佛会灵塔、塔林遗址等。

Minquan Baiyun Temple

Located at Baiyunsi Village of Yindian, Minquan County, the temple was originally Baiyi Nunnery, built during Tang Emperor Zhenguan's Reign (627-649). It was repaired and expanded during the Ming and Qing dynasties. Skanda, Arhat, and Mahavira Halls, stone pillars with inscription, Iron Bell, etc. are preserved.

崇法寺塔

位于永城县城东北烈士陵园内，始建于宋绍圣二年（1095年），绍圣五年（1098年）落成；为八角楼阁式九层砖塔，高34.6米；整体由地宫、塔基、塔身、塔刹四部分组成。塔身第一层四面辟圭形门，北面内设盘旋踏道可拾级而上，塔心室设在第五、六层，塔顶有覆钵、相轮、伞盖、宝瓶组成的塔刹。

Yongcheng Chongfa Temple Pagoda

Located in Martyrs' Park in Yongcheng County, it was built between 1095 and 1098. The 34.6-meter-high pavilion-style octagonal brick pagoda has nine floors and a spire.

圣寿寺塔

位于睢县后台乡阎庄村东北，建于北宋；平面六角形，九级密檐式砖塔，高22米；除第一层檐下置一斗三升斗拱外，其余各层皆为叠涩塔檐；第一层内为六角形塔心室，二层以上为实心，第六、八层塔身门面辟有圭形门。塔顶有覆钵、宝珠、宝瓶组成的塔刹。

Shengshou Temple Pagoda

Located northeast of Yanzhuang Village of Houtaixiang, Suixian County, and built during the Northern Song Dynasty. The nine-floor hexagonal brick pagoda, with dense eaves and a spire atop is 22 meters high. Buddha figures with varied expressions inlay the indoor walls.

无忧寺塔

位于睢县平岗镇周塔村北，为宋仿唐建筑，平面呈八角形，楼阁式砖塔，顶部已毁。现存三级，残高11米。第一层塔心室为方形，顶部用砖雕斗拱组成藻井，古朴大方。塔角处均为圆形倚柱，外壁有直棂窗。塔北面有梯道可盘旋登攀。

Wuyou Temple Pagoda
This Tang-style temple was built during the Song Dynasty (960-1279) north of Zhouta Village, Pinggang Town, Suixian County. The top of the pavilion-style octagonal brick pagoda was destroyed. The existing part is 11 meters high. It can be climbed via spiral stairs on the north side.

| 双状元塔 |

位于民权县双塔乡双塔集北门小学院内。双塔东西并列，八棱十三层，砖石叠砌而成，为纪念宋痒、宋祁兄弟在宋天圣二年（1024年）同举甲子科进士而建。

Dual-Champion Pagodas of Minquan County

Located at Shuangta Jibeimen Primary School in Shuangta Village, Minquan County, the two Pagodas stand side-by-side in the east to west. The 13-floor octagonal brick and stone pagodas honor the success of brothers Song Yang and Song Qi becoming imperial examination scholars in the second year of Song Tiansheng's Reign in 1024.

八关斋会报德记碑亭

位于商丘南郊北刘庄村东,《八关斋会报德记》全称《有唐宋州官吏八关斋会报德记》。碑为青石质八棱柱形,高 2.7 米,每面宽 0.5 米,唐大历七年(772 年)立。碑文楷书,著名书法家颜真卿撰文并书写,记述田神功抵御安史之乱的功绩和八关斋会盛况。明嘉靖时期(1522~1566 年)加盖碑亭。

Eight Precepts Association Moral Report Pavilion

Situated in the east of Liuzhuang Village in southern suburb of Shangqiu, it was created and wrote by the famous calligrapher Yan Zhenqing in 772 to describe the merits of Tian Shengong fighting against the rebellion of An Lushan and Shi Siming, and the spectacular events of Eight Precepts Association. The pavilion was built from 1522 to 1566.

侯府

位于商丘古城内，是明末户部尚书候恂的故居。现存堂楼一座，堂屋一座，均为青砖灰瓦，雕花门窗，硬山式建筑。候恂，字若谷，是《桃花扇》的主人公侯方域之父，明万历四十四年（1616年）进士，文武全才，为官清廉，被誉为"东林党党魁"。

Hou Mansion

Located in the ancient city of Shangqiu, Hou Mansion was the ancestral residence of Hou Xun, an important late Ming official. The extant flush gable roof-style black brick, grey tile building and central hall has carved doors and windows. Hou Xun, a scholar who passed the imperial examination in 1616 during Ming Emperor Wanli's Reign was an upright official of literary and military capacity.

| 壮悔堂 |

位于商丘县城刘隅首东一街,建于明末,清代重修。为明末才子侯方域幼年读书处,原名杂佣堂。侯氏35岁旧地重游,痛悔一事无成而改名壮悔堂,并发愤著述。现存过厅、壮悔堂、香君楼、翡翠楼,保存完好,其中壮悔堂面阔五间,进深二间,硬山灰瓦顶二层楼房,前出廊。

Hall of Remorse for Youth

Located at Liuyushou East First Street in Shangqiu, the Hall of Remorse for the Young was built in the late Ming Dynasty. Here Hou Fangyu, a gifted scholar, studied in his childhood. He revisited the place at 35 years old and felt regret that he had not accomplished more; so, he renamed it Hall of Remorse for Youth to show his regret. The extant buildings include Vestibule, Plum Blossom Hall, Fragrance Building and Jade Building.

> 穆氏四合院

　　位于商丘市睢阳区古城内的中山东二街路南，为信奉道教的穆家宅院，前后三进四合院，保存完好。有过厅、正房、后楼、东、西厢房等建筑，硬山灰瓦顶，透花木雕，隔扇门窗。

Mu Clan Quadrangle Courtyard

The courtyard, which is located south of Zhongshan East Second Street in Suiyang District, Shangqiu, belonged to the Mu family who followed Taoism. The courtyard has vestibules, main house, rear building and wing rooms with wood carved decorations, doors and windows.

睢县东关清真寺

位于睢县城东关，始建于元代中期。现存建筑多为明、清风格，坐西向东，以拜殿为中心，周围有门楼、讲堂、善堂、浴室等。蓝砖绿瓦，飞檐花壁，木雕装饰，气势恢宏。1947年，华东野战军司令员粟裕大将曾在这里指挥睢杞战役

Dongguan Mosque of Suixian County

The mosque, in Dongguan in Suixian County, is more than 600 years old; its extant structures were mostly built in the Ming and Qing style. The worship hall stands at the middle of the mosque flanked by Gateway, Lecture and Charity Halls.

宁陵清真寺

位于宁陵县城关镇东关村，始建于元末明初，后世曾多次扩建和重修。由门楼、对厅、大殿、望月楼、南北两院五大部分组成，寺内建筑结构严谨，布局巧妙，层次分明，木雕砖雕精巧别致，独具特色。

Yuan Dynasty Ningling Mosque
The mosque, dating back over 600 years, is located at Dongguan Village of Guanzhen, Ningling County. It has gateway, halls, Moon Watching Tower and courtyards in the south and north.

商丘天主教堂

位于商丘古城中山南二街,清光绪三十三年(1907年)由意大利米兰外方传教会来华传教士谭维新(开封教区主教)创办,原系河南省开封教区的一个本堂区,1924年先后建大小楼房五座,210余间,占地9400平方米,共有五个院落。

Shangqiu Catholic Church
The church at Zhongshan South Second Street in Shangqiu was established in 1907 by Italian missionary Tan Weixin, it has five buildings and five courtyards.

圣保罗医院

位于商丘市睢阳区北关。1915年，加拿大籍医生将建在开封的"三一"圣公会教会医院迁至商丘，1917年扩建称圣保罗医院，系淮海战役总前委后勤机关旧址所在地，现为商丘市第一人民医院。建筑飞檐挑角，另有讲堂等建筑共七座，附设地下室，占地两万平方米。

St. Paul Hospital

The Hospital is at Beiguan of Suiyang District, Shangqiu. A Canadian doctor relocated the "31" Church Hospital from Kaifeng to Shangqiu in 1915 and renamed it St. Paul Hospital after an expansion in 1917. It is now the Shangqiu First People's Hospital. It has a number of buildings such as the Lecture Hall.

毛泽东视察黄楼纪念馆

位于商丘市梁园区北五千米处,纪念馆分设大厅和四个展厅。1958年,毛泽东同志到此处视察,为此,商丘人民于1961年建造"毛主席视察黄楼纪念亭"和1968年建造的"毛主席视察黄楼纪念馆"。

Mao Zedong Memorial Hall

The hall, 5,000 meters north of Liangyuan District, Shangqiu, was built in memory of Chairman Mao's visit in 1958. It consists of a main hall and four exhibition halls.

> 中共中原局扩大会议旧址

　　位于商丘市睢阳区中山西二街,原为中华圣公会礼拜堂,西洋教会建筑,共有房六间,坐南面北。会议厅面阔24.9米,进深13.2米。1949年在此召开中共中原局扩大会议,会议传达了中共中央七届二中全会精神,部署了渡江作战计划。

Expanded Meeting Site of the Central Plains Bureau of the Central Committee

The meeting site, located at Zhongshan West Second Street in Suiyang District, Shangqiu, had been the Chinese Anglican Church. The Western church-style building has six rooms. The meeting was held here in 1949.

39

中共中央中原局扩大会议秘书处旧址

位于淮阳区党校院内，整体为青砖灰瓦硬山式清代建筑。现存房屋最南一座是秘书处工作人员办公地点，青砖灰瓦，硬山式建筑。北两排为单间，为工作人员住地。

Secretariat of the Expanded Meeting Site of the Central Plains Bureau of the Central Committee

Located at the Suiyang District Party School, the black brick, grey tile Qing Dynasty existing houses include the southernmost secretariat staff office; two rows of houses in the north are single staff quarters.

陈官庄淮海战役纪念馆

　　位于永城市东北25千米陈官庄。1949年1月6日下午，中原、华东野战军及地方武装60余万人对驻扎在陈官庄一线的国民党军队发起总攻，激战96小时，全歼国民党军20余万人，淮海战役宣告胜利结束。现村内建有淮海战役陈官庄歼敌纪念馆，村北有陈官庄烈士陵园，安葬着1600名烈士。

Chenguanzhuang Huaihai Campaign Memorial

The memorial is located at Chenguanzhuang, 25 kilometers northeast of Yongcheng. The Chinese People's Liberation Army fiercely battled the Kuomintang troops here on 6th January 1949 and won a victory.

彭雪枫纪念馆

　　位于夏邑县城东 16 千米的八里庄村，建于 1944 年，纪念馆里展陈彭雪枫生平事迹。彭雪枫（1907～1944 年），中共早期党员，曾任新四军四师师长兼淮北军区司令员，1944 年 9 月 11 日在八里庄与日伪战斗中殉国。

Peng Xuefeng Memorial
Situated at Balizhuang Village, 16 kilometers east of Xiayi County, it was built in 1944 in memory of Peng Xuefeng, who died for his country on 11th September 1944.

夏邑二鬼摔跤

　　二鬼摔跤或称"二娃摔跤""二喜摔跤",是中原传统民间舞蹈,已流传上百年。表演者背驮二鬼摔跤道具,通过表演者腿、背、臂等综合协调动作,给观众以两个"鬼"在摔跤的外观表现。常在农历七月十五、清明节、庙会等逢会节日时进行表演。

Two Ghosts Wrestling of Xiayi

It is a traditional dance of the Central Plains that has been passed down for hundreds of years. Usually it is performed in Lunar July 15th, Qingming Festival, temple fair and other festivals.

李秀山泥塑

商丘柘城县远襄镇的李秀山泥塑属家族传承,始于清末民初,系民间庙堂彩塑的传承技艺。泥塑人物多为民俗生活一类,形象生动,生活气息浓郁。

Clay Sculpture of Li Xiushan

It is a family inheritance originated from the late Qing Dynasty and early Republic of China. As the techniques of colored sculpture of temples, the figures of clay sculpture mostly present the vivid and lively folk life. Clay sculpture of Li Xiushan has been included in the first batch of Intangible Cultural Heritage of Henan Province.

夏邑县火店镇灯笼村

位于夏邑县火店镇,该处的灯笼加工有近千年的历史。生产的宫灯、旗穗、排须、中国结、刺绣等产品驰名海内外,宫灯曾挂到北京天安门城楼和人民大会堂。近年对其不断改造、创新,种类不断丰富。

Lantern Village, Huodian Town Xiayi County

This village, where Lantern production dates back nearly one thousand years, produces palace lanterns, tassels, fringes, Chinese knots and embroidery famous in China and abroad.

永城市茴村镇书法村

永城市茴村民风淳朴，人们崇尚书法，全镇 5000 多人中有 1000 多人是常年习练的书法爱好者，是远近闻名的"书法村"。

Calligraphy Village in Huicun Town, Yongcheng

In well-known Calligraphy Village, one fifth of the population is calligraphy lovers who practice it year-round.

民权县农民画

民权县北关镇王公村地处黄河故道,全村1300多人中500多人从事绘画产业,夫妻画家、父子画家、姐妹画家以及三世同堂画家比比皆是,年绘画作品两万余幅。他们以画虎为主,兼画人物、花鸟、山水等,品种繁多。

Farmers' Paintings of Minquan County

Wanggong Village of Beiguan Town in Minquan County is located on the old course of the Yellow River. Here nearly half the population engages in the drawing with an annual output of over 20,000 paintings. Though tigers are the main subjects, their paintings include or traits, flowers, birds and landscapes.

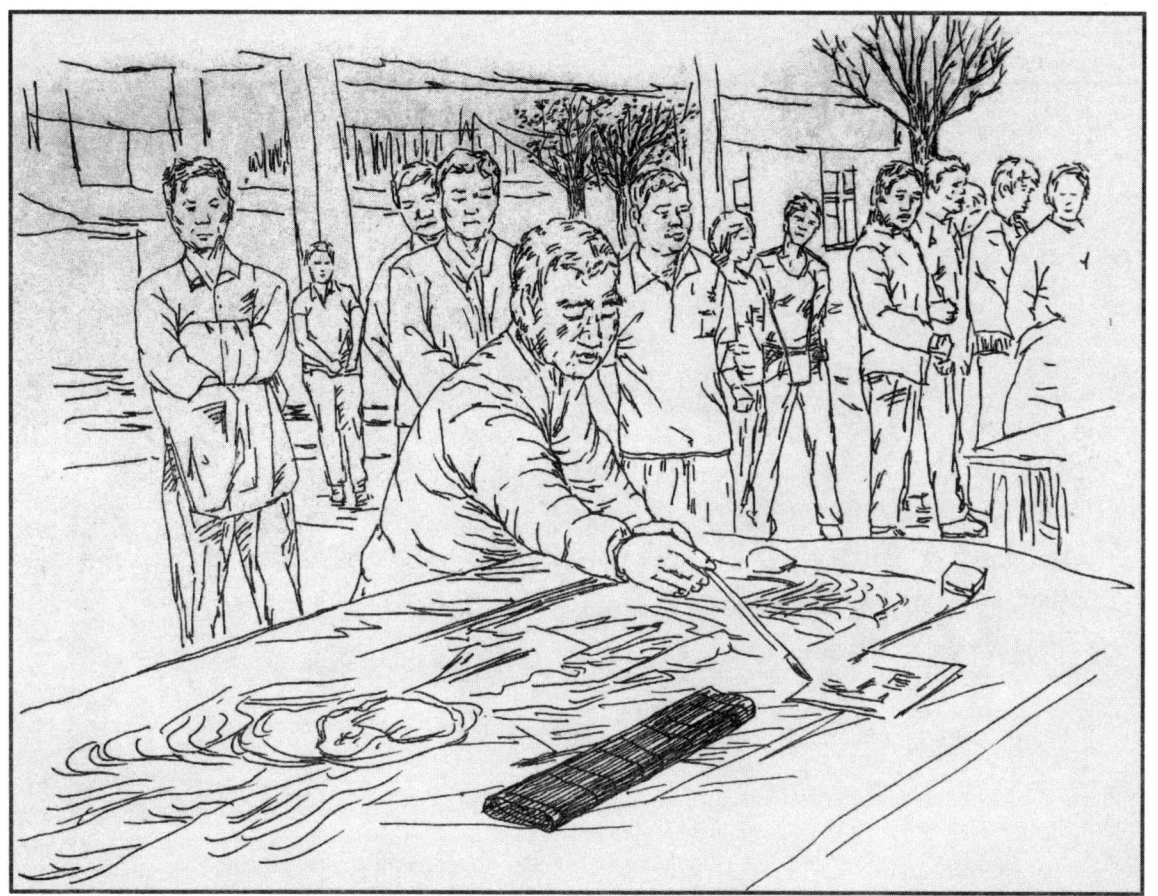

火神台庙会

亦称阏伯台、火星台，位于商丘古城西南 1.5 千米火星台村。台高 35 米，周长 270 米，为夯土堆积而成。会期从春节后开始，正月初七是火神的生日，此天人最多，延续整个正月。庙会在睢阳古城南门外的火神台景区和遂皇陵景区内进行。

Temple Fair in Stand of God of Fire

Temple fairs are held after the Chinese Spring Festival and last throughout the first lunar month at Huoxingtai Village, 1.5 kilometers southwest of Shangqiu. The seventh day of the first lunar month is the birthday of the God of Fire. Most people attended the fair on this day.

四平调

源于民间花鼓。男挎花鼓、击节打花，女顶绣球、足踩高跷，两人席地对唱。因它以花鼓为主，吸收评剧、京剧、梆子等剧种的曲调而形成，有人便称它为"四拼调"，后改称"四平调"。四平调是中国民间艺术中的一朵奇葩。

Siping Tune

Siping Tune, originating from the folk flower-drum, has a man beating a rhythm on a flower-drum and a woman walking on stilts with an embroidered ball on her head while both sing in antiphonal style. With flower-drum as a key element, Siping Tune has a basis in many drama tunes.

麒麟舞

　　睢县麒麟舞鼻祖是明末掌管宫廷文化娱乐的冯玮，归隐故里后将其传授给大刘寨村的冯氏族众，至今已传15世，有300多年历史。道具为麒麟头、麒麟皮和绣球。表演技巧有十多种，传统表演形式分为"盘门""平地表演""桌上表演"三段。麒麟为中国古代传说中的一种吉祥的神兽。

Unicorn Dance

Suixian County Unicorn Dance originated from the Ming Dynasty and has been passed on for 15 generations for more than 300 years. With unicorn head and skin and embroidered balls as props, the showmanship is diverse. Unicorns are ancient Chinese legendary lucky god animals.

开封市
Kaifeng City

> 开封城墙

　　开封城墙是以唐建中二年（781年）重建的汴州城为基础，经后世重修和扩建逐渐形成的。现存为清道光二十二年（1842年）重建的遗存，周长14.4千米，高7.6米，顶宽5米，城墙马面保存尚好。南大门内立有清道光二十四年（1844年）"重修河南省城碑记"碑刻一通。

Kaifeng City Walls
Kaifeng City Walls were rebuilt and expanded on the basis of Bianzhou, a city rebuilt in 781. The existing well-preserved walls built in 1842 have a perimeter of 14.4 kilometers and are 7.6 meters high and five meters wide.

龙亭

位于开封城内西北隅,原为宋、金皇宫故址,明初在其上建周王府,清代扩建为万寿宫。现存重檐歇山顶大殿一座,坐落在高 13.4 米的台基之上,大殿东侧有一石坊,上有康有为 1923 年游龙亭题诗。亭前大道左右有潘湖和杨湖。龙亭南数十米处有一面照壁,前有山门。午朝门前有宋代石狮一对,清代碑刻数通。

Dragon Pavilion

Located at the northwest corner of Kaifeng, Dragon Pavilion was a site of Golden Palace. A Hall with double eaves and gable and hip roof has been preserved. An avenue in front of the pavilion goes through Pan Lake and Yang Lake. Screen wall, monastery gate, stone lions of the Song Dynasty and steles of the Qing Dynasty are still preserved in front of the pavilion.

开封府文庙

始建于清顺治四年（1647年），康熙年间（1662～1722年）多次重修。现仅存棂星门，门楼为木牌楼，三门三开，施斗拱五朵，朱门绿瓦，四根通天柱顶蹲踞四兽，门前一对石狮，保存尚好。

Kaifeng Confucius Temple

Built in 1647 it underwent repairs during Qing Emperor Kangxi's Reign (1662-1722). Only Lingxing Gate Tower and a pair of stone lions are still preserved in front of the gate tower.

铁塔

始建于北宋皇祐元年（1049年），本名开宝寺塔，因外壁镶嵌褐色琉璃塔砖，其色似铁，故俗称铁塔。八角十三层砖雕建筑，雕砖刻有飞天、坐佛、菩萨、伎乐、祥禽、瑞兽、花卉等。底层四面辟圭形门，北面设梯道可盘旋至顶。

Iron Tower

Originally named Kaibao Pagoda, construction began 1049. It was later named Iron Tower because the color of brown glazed bricks on the outer walls looks like iron. The 13-floor octagonal brick tower is decorated with carved animals, flowers and Buddha images.

| 相国寺 |

始建于北齐天保六年（555年），现存为清乾隆三十一年（1766年）重建。中轴线自南而北依次为天王殿，内有彩塑四大金刚；大雄宝殿、罗汉殿、藏经楼及东、西阁等。大门东侧钟亭有巨钟一口，清乾隆三十三年（1768年）铸，重约五吨，钟声悠扬。门前另有一对威武的石狮。

Xiangguo Temple

The Temple was built in 555; its existing part was built in 1766 during Qing Emperor Qianlong's Reign. The hall of Heavenly Guardians, Mahavira Hall, Arhats Hall and the Depository of Buddhist Sutras are situated on the central axis of the Temple. Bell Pavilion has a huge bell weighing about five tons.

繁塔

原名兴慈塔，因其地称繁台，俗称繁塔，始建于宋开宝七年（974年）。原为六角九层楼阁式砖塔，后因遭雷击，明拆除三层以上部分，清初增建为七层实心小塔，形成塔上有塔。塔高33.68米，内外壁镶嵌数以千计的佛像砖，千姿百态。塔内存约200方宋至清历代碑刻，十分精美。

Fan Tower

Formerly called Xingci Tower, it was later known as Fan Tower. A hexagonal pavilion-style nine- floor tower was built in 974, but the existing one is a smaller seven-floor solid tower 34 meters high. Inlaid with thousands of bricks with Buddha images and about 200 stone inscriptions of different dynasties it is well preserved.

延庆观

位于古城东北屏风山上，因建成于延庆元年（1124年）而得名，明嘉靖二十八年（1549年）重修。现仅存三层玉皇阁，高13米，底层正方形中空；中层八角实心，用绿色琉璃瓦砌成人字形山墙；上层为八角攒尖顶亭，精美异常。

Yanqing Taoist Temple

Located at Pingfeng Mountain in northeast of ancient Kaifeng, the temple was built in 1124. Only three layers of Pavilion of Jade Emperor still exist. The pavilion is 13 meters high, the middle layer is solid and octagonal; a top is an octagonal spire pavilion.

太平兴国寺

位于尉氏县城东关，始建于北宋太平兴国年间（976～983年），后历经维修，塔高30米，为六角八层楼阁式砖塔，内可盘旋而上。内外壁均镶嵌有佛像，檐下置砖雕仿木斗拱。顶层有明嘉靖二十五年（1546年）"重修宝塔顶三层"题记一则。

Taiping Xingguo Temple

Built during the Northern Song Dynasty Taiping Xingguo's reign (976-983) in Weishi County, the eight-floor hexagonal, brick 30-meter tower is and inlaid with Buddha images inside and out.

杞县大云寺塔

位于杞县南25千米瓦岗村，始建于唐末，明代重建，为八角七级楼阁式砖塔，高19.3米。塔身各层均砌叠涩塔檐，一层西面辟门可入塔心室，塔心室内嵌佛像雕砖，外壁嵌云朵、花卉、鸟兽图案雕砖。三层以上为实心，塔身内外共嵌佛像400余尊。

Dayun Temple Tower, Qixian County

The octagonal, pavilion-style brick tower in Wagang Village, 25 kilometers south of Qixian County is more than 1,000 years old. The 19.3-meter, seven-storey tower has over 400 inlaid Buddha images.

开封东大寺

　　始建年代不详，现存建筑为清道光二十六年（1846年）重修。坐西朝东，占地6050平方米，中轴线自东而西为大门面阔五间，二门，左右廊房、讲堂、水房，中为大殿，均为硬山灰瓦顶。有明代阿拉伯文可兰经文碑记清康熙二十八年（1689年）重建清真寺碑各一通。

Kaifeng East Temple
The extent temple was rebuilt in 1846, but its initial construction date is unknown. The temple faces east with entrance door, bungalow, lecture hall and main hall on the central axis. They all have gabled roofs of grey tile.

北清真寺

现存建筑为清道光二十年（1840年）重修。占地1534平方米，坐西朝东，中轴线上自东而西依次为大门、南北厢房各六间、卷棚、二殿、大殿、后窑殿。寺内有清代碑刻四通（含有包拯"龙马负图处"一通）。

North Mosque

The existing North Mosque was rebuilt in 1840. It faces east and has an entrance door, wing rooms, round ridge roof, Second, Main and Rear Halls on its central axis. There are four Qing Dynasty inscriptions in the mosque.

朱仙镇岳飞庙

建于明成化十四年（1478年），坐北朝南，现存建筑面积5000平方米。山门面阔三间，东西厢房各五间，大殿面阔五间，进深三间，单檐歇山式绿琉璃瓦顶。殿前有明代碑刻八通，其中有摹刻的岳飞手迹《送紫屋张先生北伐》碑、《满江红》碑，具有极高的历史和书法艺术价值。

Yuefei Temple, Zhuxian Town

The temple, built in 1478, faces south and has a monastery gate, wing rooms and main halls. In front of the main hall are eight Ming Dynasty inscriptions of great historic and artistic value.

山陕甘会馆

建于清乾隆四十一年（1776年），是清代客居开封的山西、陕西、甘肃同乡联谊之所。坐北朝南，前有照壁，后有钟、鼓楼东西对峙，中轴线上有一座六柱三间五楼式牌坊，后为拜殿，另有厢房，侧院。整个建筑布满了砖雕、石雕、木雕，十分精美，有很高的艺术价值。

Shanxi-Shaanxi-Gansu Guild Hall

Built in 1776, the hall was for gatherings of countrymen from Shanxi, Shaanxi and Gansu provinces who lived in Kaifeng during the Qing Dynasty. The south-facing hall has screen walls, opera tower, Bell and Drum Tower and main hall. It is decorated with brick, stone and woodcarvings.

[孟子游梁祠]

位于开封包公湖一带,始建于北宋,是为纪念孟子到魏国国都大梁游学而建。明初重建,大殿六楹,中祀孟子,左右为其弟子,后被淹毁。清顺治十二年(1655年),被移建在新府学明伦堂之后,名游梁书院。后又重建游梁祠及书院,现存残碑两通。

Mencius Temple

The temple, located alongside Kaifeng's Baogong Lake, was built about a thousand years ago in memory of Mencius' study tour in the State of Wei. The existing temple built in the early Ming Dynasty. In 1655 it was relocated to Minglun Hall(a place for reading, teaching and research) and renamed Youliang Academy.

| 无梁庙 |

　　位于开封龙亭东湖东侧,始建于清乾隆年间(1736～1795年),后曾重修,坐北向南,整个建筑无梁无柱,故曰无梁庙。主体建筑为大殿,下方上圆,为叠涩收顶的传统建筑造型。系道教庙宇,内祀火神、关帝(武财神)和大王(河神)三尊神像。

Wuliang Temple

Located east of Kaifeng's Longtingdong Lake, it was built during Qing Emperor Qianlong's Reign(1736-1795). Facing south, the temple has neither beams nor columns. The main hall, round at the top, square at the bottom, honors three Taoist idols.

禹王台

位于开封市东南隅，占地26万平方米，台上有纪念大禹治水功绩的禹王庙。禹王庙正殿东院为三贤祠，祠内原有李白、杜甫、高适的塑像，明嘉靖（1522～1566年）时增祀李梦阳、何景明两位明朝诗人。正殿西院为水德祠，前为御书楼，上悬乾隆御题"功在河洛"匾额。

Yuwang Platform

The platform, at the southeast corner of Kaifeng, was built at Yuwang Temple in memory of the achievements of Yu the Great in controlling floods. Sanxian Temple lies in the eastern courtyard of the temple's main hall and the statues of three great Tang poets -Li Bai, Du Fu and Gao Shi, are honored here.

镇河铁犀

位于开封城东北铁牛村,犀高约两米,独角朝天,为明代政治家于谦督铸。明洪武二十年(1387年)和永乐八年(1410年)黄河在开封两次决口,酿成灾祸。于谦奉命治理,于正统十一年(1446年)铸成铁犀,并亲撰《镇河铁犀铭》铸在犀背。镇河铁犀表达了人民要求根除河患的强烈愿望。

River-Guarding Iron Rhinoceros

Located at Tieniu Village in the northeast Kaifeng, the rhinoceros is about two meters high. The Yellow River burst twice at Kaifeng in 1387 and 1410 bringing disaster to the people. Yu Qian, entrusted with a mission to harness the Yellow River, made an iron rhinoceros to show his determination to prevent disaster.

河南贡院

原址位于河南大学外语学院北侧。贡院最早始于唐朝，是会试的考场。清光绪二十九年（1903年）、三十年（1904年）全国会试在河南贡院举行，科举制度在这里划上句号，随后在此基础上建立河南大学。现存碑刻两通，清雍正十年（1732年）年所立《改建河南贡院碑》和清道光二十四年（1844年）所立《重修河南贡院碑记》。

Henan Examination Hall

Henan Examination Hall lies north of the Foreign Language Institute of Henan University. It was built during the Tang Dynasty. National examinations were held here in 1903 and 1904, drawing an end to the Chinese ancient imperial exam system.

河南大学·博雅楼

图为河南大学的博雅楼，位于明伦校区中轴线西侧，亦称七号楼。它是一座中西合璧的建筑，楼高三层，连同地下室共四层，总建筑面积为4000多平方米。20世纪20年代，博雅楼建成并投入使用，曾作为河南留学欧美预备学校和中州大学时期的教学活动中心，现在仍在发挥作用。

Henan University (1)

The sketch shows Henan University's Boya Building. West side of Henan University Minglun Campus' central axis, it has Chinese and Western architectural styles. Built in the 1920s, it has three stories and a basement.

| 河南大学·大礼堂 |

　　1931年由时任校长的许心武提出决议，张清廉教授设计，历时三年而成。南北长73.75米，东西宽53.75米，总建筑面积4687平方米，大礼堂内部分上下两层，共可容近3000人，另设有休息、音乐储藏和道具化妆等房间，大门有八根爱奥尼式立柱。礼堂至今仍在使用。

Henan University (2)
The sketch shows the university's auditorium built in 1934. The two-storey building is 73.75 meters south to north and 53.75 meters east to west. Eight Ionic columns stand at the two sides of the door. The auditorium seats nearly 3,000 people.

本笃修女会会堂

位于开封市自由路中段路北,由著名的留美建筑师杨廷宝设计,建于1937年,原系天主教美国本笃修女会设于开封的会址。该建筑系两层中国仿古楼房,曾为日本驻开封领事馆,现为开封宾馆二号楼。该建筑平面为U形,坡屋面,灰瓦歇山顶。

Bendu Sisters Hall

Located in the middle section of Kaifeng's Ziyou Road, the all was built in 1937. The two-storey Chinese arched hall on a U-shaped plane, used to be the Japanese consulate in Kaifeng. Now it is the second reception building of Kaifeng Hotel.

朱仙镇清真寺

位于朱仙镇东南隅,始建于明代,清乾隆三年(1737年)重修,是开封境内现存最大的一座伊斯兰教清真寺。清真寺坐西向东,现存建筑有山门、南北厢房及大殿等。厢房内有碑楼两座,一座内存乾隆三十二年(1767年)所刻清真古行正教条例;另一座内存嘉庆十年(1805年)所刻阿拉伯文碑。

Zhuxian Town Mosque

The mosque is at Zhuxian's southeast corner. Built during the Ming Dynasty and restored in 1737, facing east, the mosque still has the original gate, south-north wing rooms and main hall. The wing rooms house two stele pavilions.

> 开封市天主教堂

位于开封市理事厅街，占地 6000 多平方米，1917 年由意大利传教士谭维新主教主持而建，哥特式建筑。现存礼拜堂一座，其旁有尖塔顶钟楼。1948 年 6 月，开封解放时，解放军攻入城后指挥部设于此。现为开封市规模最大的一座天主教堂。

Catholic Church of Kaifeng
Situated on Kaifeng's Lishiting Street, it was established in 1917 by Italian missionary Tan Weixin. The gothic-style church with chapel and pinnacle clock tower is Kaifeng's largest Catholic church.

天主教河南总修道院

位于开封市东郊的羊尾铺村，又称"天主教河南神哲学院"，是培训神职人员的场所。天主教河南总修院经罗马教廷传信部批准办学，1932年建成。现存建筑主要有大门、主楼和小教堂。主楼为中西合璧的高两层的环形建筑，占地2700平方米。整体外观为中国古典式，内部为西式装饰。

Henan Catholic Monastery

The monastery, at Yangweipu Village in Kaifeng's eastern suburbs, was built in 1932. The existing building includes the entrance door, main building and chapel. The circular main building has Chinese and Western architectural styles.

陈留天主教堂

位于陈留镇西街，1921年美、英传教士修建，中西合璧建筑。原有25间房屋，后部分改建。现存礼拜堂、后楼等建筑14间。后楼系地上两层，地下一层，年久失修，濒临坍塌。

Chenliu Catholic Church

Located at West Street in Chenliu, the church was built in 1921 by American and British missionaries in Chinese and Western architectural styles. There are 14 buildings including a chapel.

禹王台红楼

位于禹王台公园西侧,建于清光绪三十年(1904年),是当时承建汴洛铁路工程的比利时和法国工程技术人员的宿舍楼,以红色为主调,又称红楼。该楼主楼坐东向西,面阔五间、进深一间、楼高两层。"中原大战"期间,冯玉祥在此设立战地医院,后来作为河南大学农学院图书馆使用。

Yuwang Platform "Red Building"

The "Red Building" is west of Yuwang Platform Park. It was built in 1904 as a dormitory for Belgian and French staff constructing the Kaifeng-Luoyang railway. The west facing "red" building is now the library of the Agriculture Institute of Henan University.

国共"黄河归故"谈判旧址

位于禹王台区民生街,1917年由当时北京邮政总局拨款而建。位于东面的红洋楼系邮务长阿良西公寓,楼后有六间附属用房及小院,建筑为巴洛克式风格。抗战胜利后为联合国救济总署所在地。1946年7月19日,周恩来自上海到开封,与国民党当局谈判解决"黄河归故"问题时下榻于此。

Nationalist and Communist Negotiation Site
Located at Minsheng Street in Yuwang Platform District, it was built in 1917. Baroque style Hongyang Building, on the east, has six subsidiary rooms and small a courtyard behind. Zhou Enlai stayed at here in July 1946.

兴隆火车站旧址

位于祥符区兴隆乡北部陇海铁路北,由火车站站舍、站长住所、防空洞组成。火车站站舍始建于1913年,为比利时人所建比利时风格的宫殿庙宇式建筑,面积约171平方米。20世纪30年代中期,日本人再建日式风格站长住所、防空洞,见证了中国铁路火车站站舍的历史,具有较高的历史研究价值。

Xinglong Railway Station

Located north of Longhai Railway in Xinglong, Xiangfu District, the railway station was built in 1913. It is Belgian palace and temple style. In the mid 1930s, the Japanese built a Japanese-style residence and air-raid shelter.

刘青霞故居

位于开封市顺河回族区北土街刘家胡同。刘青霞（1877～1922年），清两广巡抚马丕瑶之女，著名社会活动家、教育家、政治家。早期同盟会成员，创办了河南的第一所女校，辛亥革命后任北京女子政法大学校长等职。旧居为一四合院，清末建筑，现存硬山灰瓦房16间。

Liu Qingxia's Former Residence

The residence is at Liujia Alley of Beitu Street in the Hui Ethnic Community of Kaifeng's Shunhe District. Liu Qingxia (1877-1922), a member of the Chinese Revolutionary League in its early times, founded the first girls' school in Henan Province. The existing residence is a quadrangle courtyard with 16 rooms and a grey tile gabled roof.

华北体育场旧址

位于开封龙亭北路,原为河南省公共体育场,1932年因在此举办第十六届华北运动会,又名华北体育场。1931年9月建成,占地8.19万平方米,设田径场、球类场、八级看台、办公大楼及南大门等。现仅存南大门,为四柱三券砖混结构门楼,券门上有砖砌主楼和次楼,主券门上主楼高约八米。

North China Stadium Site

Located north of Longting Road in Kaifeng, the Stadium was built in 1931. The 16th Sports Games of North China was held here in 1932. The stadium consisted of track and ballgame fields, stands, office building and South Gate. Only the South Gate remains.

刘少奇在开封陈列馆

位于开封市北土街 10 号，原为 1928 年建造的"同合裕银号"。1969 年 10 月 17 日晚，原中共中央副主席、国家主席刘少奇在这里逝世，1993 年 8 月辟为刘少奇在开封陈列馆，1994 年 11 月 12 日对外开放。

Liu Shaoqi Exhibition Hall in Kaifeng
#10 Beitu Street in Kaifeng, is where Liu Shaoqi, former Vice Chairman, Central Committee of the Communist Party and former Chinese president, died in 1969. It became an exhibition hall for Liu Shaoqi in 1993.

田家宅院

位于顺河回族区乐观街，相传为清代望族田氏家宅，田家曾出三个进士。原为三进四合院，现仅存一院，坐北朝南，正屋面阔三间，进深三间，前出轩，檐下有云龙、荷花透雕雀替，室内有雕花槅扇。东西厢房各三间，硬山灰瓦顶。大门上方原有清代"进士第"匾额，现已无存。

Tian Clan Residence

A legendary residence of the distinguished Qing Dynasty Tian family, one quadrangle courtyard with main building and east-and west-wing-rooms survives. Inside are exquisite carvings.

开封盘鼓

开封盘鼓起源于古代军队中流行的讶鼓鼓乐,气势宏大、震撼人心,鼓点激越,复杂多变;表演热烈、粗犷、豪放,无沦是在音乐性上还是在舞蹈性上都有极强的艺术表现力和感染力。因此,开封盘鼓深受人民群众的喜爱、久盛不衰。

Kaifeng Drum

Kiafeng Drum, originated from the military drum in ancient times, has grand momentum that excites the mind of people. It shows dense and loud drumbeats in complicated and variable ways. The bold, unrestrained and passionate performance, regardless the music or dance, is of extreme artistic expression and infectivity.

开封风筝

开封风筝制作工艺传承历史已有数千年,制作种类繁多,做工考究。每逢春季,古城上空风筝纷飞,争奇斗艳。近年来,开封先后承办了全国第二届风筝比赛和国际风筝会,使这一传统的民俗活动不断发扬光大。

Kiafeng Kites

The kite production techniques of Kaifeng can be traced back to thousands of years ago. It has numerous production varieties and exquisite workmanship. In every spring there will be countless kites flying in the air of this ancient town to contend in beauty and fascination.

大相国寺梵乐

　　梵乐又称佛乐或梵呗,是佛教弘扬教法和赞颂佛、菩萨等宗教声乐。大相国寺的音乐包括"梵呗"和"劝世曲"两种,演奏乐器包括法器和乐器,法器如振金铎、木鱼、钟鼓等;乐器可单独演奏或伴奏。寺内经发掘整理诠释有106首梵乐等古乐谱,是帝王礼仪之乐的代表。

Buddhist Music at Daxiangguo Temple

Buddhist music praises the Buddha and Bodhisattvas. At Daxiangguo Temple it includes prayer chanting and cautionary songs to mankind. The temple has 106 annotated music scores.

[朱仙镇木版年画]

　　朱仙镇木版年画是中国木版年画的鼻祖，主要分布于开封朱仙镇及其周边地区。朱仙镇木版年画构图饱满，线条粗扩简炼，造型古朴夸张，色彩新鲜艳丽，为我国四大年画产地之一。

Woodblock New Year Painting Clubs, Zhuxian Town

The clubs are mainly in Kaifeng's Zhuxian Town and neighboring areas. With full composition, bold lines, primitive shapes and bright colors, Zhuxian's New Year woodblock painting is the earliest ancestor of China's woodblock new year painting.

汴京灯笼张

已有200多年历史,创始人为张泰全(1740～1806年),清光绪二十七年(1901年),慈禧太后与光绪皇帝在开封行宫住跸32天,第四代传人张弘(1839～1904年)率工匠装修、布置行宫,陈设极壮丽,张家被赞誉为"汴梁灯笼张",其制灯技艺分宫灯、走马灯、折合灯、云中灯、水中灯、造型灯等,畅销各地。

Bianjing Lantern Zhang Family

With Zhang Taiquan (1740-1806) its founder, Lantern Zhang has a history a 200-year-plus history. When Empress Dowager Cixi and Emperor Guangxu stayed in the temporary imperial palace of Kaifeng in 1901, Zhang Hong (1839-1904), 4th-generation successor of the Zhang Family, skillfully decorated the palace with his craft. The Zhangs thus won a high reputation for magnificent display. Their lanterns sell well throughout China because of the excellent construction techniques.

通许锣戏

始于唐贞观年间（627～649年），是皇帝和文武百官为了取乐而模仿天宫的仙乐编出来的宫廷戏，也叫"乐戏"。是一种以曲牌为主体的剧种，伴奏乐器以唢呐为主，配以笙、笛等及打击乐器。剧目多为历史故事戏、帝王将相戏。目前通许锣戏团还能唱30余出锣戏。唱腔粗犷、场面热烈。

Tongxu Gong Play

Gong Play from Tongxu County is a type of Qupai Style (tune names for compositions) and is more than 1,000 years old. The singing of Gong Play is bold and vigorous, with Suona, Sheng and flute in accompaniment. The Tongxu Gong Play Group performs over 30 plays.

开封斗鸡

源于北宋，每年农历正月初二及二、三、四月第一个周日进行比赛。双方把喂养的斗鸡置于"斗鸡坑"内，进行格斗。清末到民国一直在开封东门外的广场上。现在，多在龙亭公园、铁塔公园和相国寺内。斗鸡活动已成为有益于社会的体育竞技和民间娱乐活动。开封"斗鸡"被称为"国宝级名鸡"。

Kaifeng Cockfights

Originating during the Northern Song Dynasty (960-1127), Kaifeng Cock fight competition is held on the second day of the lunar January and the first Sunday in February, March and April each year. Gamecocks are put into a pit to fight. The competition is mostly held at Longting Park, Iron Pagoda Park and Xiangguo Monastery.

汴绣

又称宋绣，北宋时期已达到很高水平。据《东京梦华录》记载：东京的皇宫设有"文绣院"，徽宗年间，又设了绣画专科，将绣画分类为山水、楼阁、人物、花鸟多种类型。当时大相国寺东门外有专门的"绣巷"街。汴绣工艺品种有：单面绣、双面绣、双面异色绣、双面三异绣。

Bian Embroidery

Bian Embroidery, AKA Song Embroidery, dates back more than 1,000 years. According to historical records, the imperial palace at that time set up an Embroidery Academy and Embroidered Picture Institute and categorized embroidered pictures into various types: landscape, architecture, portrait, flowers and bird. Great varieties of arts and crafts were sold in "Embroidery Lane".

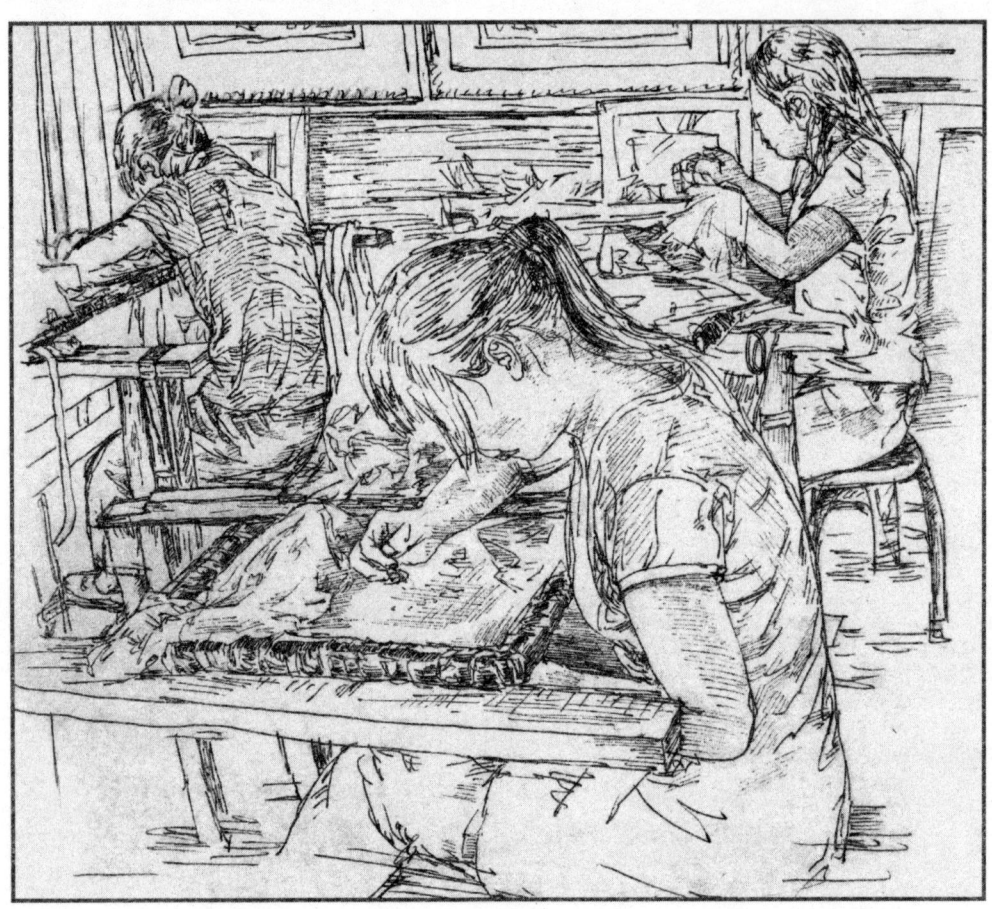

开封二夹弦

开封二夹弦起源于花鼓戏的伴奏乐器四股弦,因分别夹着弓上所系的两股马尾进行拉奏而得名,是一种稀有地方剧种,二夹弦形成于清代中期的乾隆年间(1736～1795年)。二夹弦是以说唱形式发展起来的地方剧种,演员多以唱功为主。剧目语言朴素、清新、活泼,富有浓厚的乡土气息。

Two-clip String of Kaifeng
Named after the two strings of horsetail on the bow, Kaifeng Two-clip String performs in simple language with fresh, lively and strong sense of rural breath.

摺石锁

摺石锁是一种古老的武术功力项目，产生于唐宋时期，长期在开封回族群众中广为流传。清代及民国时期，开封曾涌现出周开元、沈少三等不少摺石锁高手。开封石锁，名目繁多，花样就有数十种，是技艺和力量的完美结合，在强身健体的同时，还能给人以美的艺术享受。

Knock Lock

It is an ancient martial art program generated in the Tang (618-907) and the Song (960-1279) Dynasties, which has been widely spread among the Hui people in Kaifeng for a long time.

周口市
Zhoukou City

昆山女娲宫

位于西华县贾鲁河畔的山子头村，此地古称"昆山"。相传人祖女娲、伏羲在此"绕烟为媒，滚磨成婚"，先民为敬奉女娲而建。现存为1996年民间捐资在汉代古城遗址上所建，占地两万平方米，有女娲宫主殿和伏羲殿、玉皇殿、老母殿和两侧配殿。每逢农历初一、十五，祭祖观光者络绎不绝。

Kunshan Nüwa Palace

Legend holds that Nüwa and Fuxi, ancestors of the Chinese, got married at Shanzitou Village beside the Gulu River in Xihua County -"Kunshan" in ancient times. Ancient Chinese built the palace in memory of Nüwa. The existing palace, built in 1996, consists of Main, Fuxi and Jade Emperor Halls.

西华县女娲城

位于西华县城北的聂堆镇思都岗村。女娲是我国古代神话传说中的人类始祖,该遗址距今已有六七千年,城址呈正方形,分内外两层,城墙多为分层夯筑而成,今残存城墙最高点三米,宽八米,挖掘出大量釜、罐、鬲、瓮、瓦等春秋时期遗物。

Nüwa Town, Xihua County

Nüwa Town is in Sidugang Village, Niedui Town north of Xihua County. Nüwa is a goddess in ancient Chinese mythology best known for creating mankind. Excavation determined that Nüwa Town was square, with a maximum height at three meters and eight meters wide. A large number of Spring and Autumn Period relics were unearthed.

| 南顿故城 |

位于项城市南顿乡光武台南,是商代古城遗址。据记载为顿子国南迁至颖水南岸(今南顿),故称南顿,已有2600多年历史。现仅存一段土城墙,长217米,残高七米,顶宽五米。城内散存大量板瓦、筒瓦和饰粗细绳纹的陶片,城址内外发现有春秋和汉代墓葬。

Nandun Ancient City

Located south of Guangwutai in Nandun Village, Xiangcheng, Nandun Ancient City has over 2,600 years of history. Only a section of clay walls 217 meters in long, seven meters high and about five meters wide at the top still exist. Tombs and cultural relics were found in and around the ancient city.

太清宫

　　位于鹿邑县城东的太清宫镇，是我国古代杰出思想家、道家派创始人老子的诞生地。始建于汉延熹八年（165年），后代屡毁屡建。现存清代所修太极殿，建于高一米的台基上，南面设踏跺以供上下。大殿面阔五间，进深三间，单檐歇山黄琉璃瓦顶。殿内梁、柱、枋上施彩绘，墙上绘壁画。

Taiqing Palace

The Palace in Taiqinggong Town east of downtown Luyi, is the birthplace of Lao-Tzu, the founder of Taoism. Palace construction completed in 165 was destroyed and rebuilt many times. The existing Taiji Hall was built during the Qing Dynasty.

老君台

位于鹿邑县城老君台后街,亦称升仙台,相传老子在此成仙飞升。始建于唐天宝二年(743年),清代重建。台高八米,台顶面积706平方米,台前石阶33级,喻老子飞升三十三层青天,台上四周筑有女墙,上立24垛口,当为八卦图中24方之象征。台顶有山门、东西厢房、大殿,大殿内有老子造像碑一通。

Laojun Platform

Also called Immortal Platform, is in a Laojuntai back street in downtown Luyi, a legendary place where Lao-Tzu became an immortal. Built in 743 and restored during the Qing Dynasty. It is eight-meters high with 33 stone steps. A stele with Lao-Tzu's image stands in the main hall.

> 太昊陵

位于睢阳县城北郊蔡河北岸，相传为伏羲氏定都和长眠之地。据记载，春秋时已有陵，现存建筑多为明正统十三年（1448年）所建，庙周围外有外城、内城、紫禁城三道城垣。南北长700余米，东西宽500多米。坐北朝南，中轴线上自南而北，依次有午朝门、太极门、钟鼓楼、伏羲陵等。

Taihao Mausoleum

It is located on the Cai River in the northern suburbs of Suiyang County, which was the legendary capital and burial place of Emperor Fu Xi. Historical records show mausoleum came into existence more than 2,000 years ago and the existing structure was mostly built in 1448. Facing south, it is more than 700 meters south to north and over 500 meters east to west.

画卦台

位于淮阳县城北城湖岛上，相传为伏羲画八卦处，故又名八卦台、八卦坛。面积约4900平方米，台上存柏树一株，台前设池，相传伏羲于蔡水得白龟，掘此池放养，故名"白龟池"，现恢复八角亭一座。

Eight Diagrams Platform
Legend says the platform was where Emperor Fu Xi drew bagua, the eight combinations of three whole or broken lines used in divination. The plat form is located on a Beicheng Lake island in Huai-yang County. A cypress tree was planted on the stand. It is said that Fu Xi dug a pool in front of the stand to breed a white turtle he caught in the Cai River; so, pool was named "White Turtle Pool".

弦歌台

位于淮阳县城西南隅，旧名"绝粮祠""厄台"，传为孔子周游列国厄于陈、蔡绝粮处。东汉时陈王于此台教射，故又名"弩台"。台平面呈长方形，面积4000余平方米，高约四米。台上建筑始建于唐，现存为清代建筑。坐北朝南，依次为正门、过厅、正殿。正殿周设24根方形石柱。弦歌台三面环水，东面设甬道与岸相通。

Xiange Platform
Located at the southwest corner Huaiyang, legend holds the platform was where Confucius ate when he travelled through the area. The square stand is surrounded by water on three sides and is about four meters high. The original structure on the stand was built during the Tang Dynasty; the existing is Qing Dynasty style.

端敏袁公祠

　　位于淮阳县城。是清同治年间（1862～1874年）为袁甲三而建。袁甲三，河南项城人，袁世凯的从祖父，曾任漕运总督，谥号"端敏公"。门前有石狮一对，祠中有堂三楹，内塑神像，大门上有匾："端敏袁公祠"。东侧院有堂屋3间，房前有方塘，塘内以太湖石垒小山，塘南有耸翠亭，是文人学士吟咏胜地。现存堂三楹、张之万撰文的石碑一通。

Upright Duke Yuan's Temple

Located in the downtown of Huaiyang County, it was built to commemorate Yuan Jiasan during the Tongzhi's Reign of the Qing Dynasty (1644-1912). Yuan Jiasan, born in Xiangcheng Henan Province, was the grandfather's brother's son of Yuan Shikai. Yuan Jiasan was the governor-general of grain water transport, who got posthumous title of "Duke Upright". In front of the temple is a pair of stone lions while in the temple worships statues. There is a plaque above the gate reading "Upright Duke Yuan's Temple".

关帝庙

　　位于周口市内沙河北岸，又名山陕会馆。始建于清康熙三十二年（1693年），占地1.7万平方米。现存石碑坊、铁旗杆、碑亭、香亭、大殿、配殿、花戏楼、大拜殿、春秋阁和东西廊房102间。建筑形式有四柱三楼、六角攒尖、歇山重檐、悬山、硬山、八檩卷棚等。现存木雕、石雕、砖雕2000余幅。

Guanyu Temple

The Temple, AKA Shanxi-Shaanxi Guild Hall, is located at the north bank of the Neisha River in Zhoukou. Built in 1693, the temple has stone steles, main and side halls, playhouses and worship halls and over 2,000 wood, stone and brick carvings.

太康文庙

位于太康县城关回族镇黉学街北侧，俗称学宫，原为府学。始建于明宣德元年（1426年），清顺治五年（1648年）重建。坐北朝南，中轴线上自南而北依次为棂星门、拜殿、大成殿。拜殿面阔五间，进深三间，歇山式筒瓦顶有琉璃脊饰。大成殿建在月台上，面阔七间，进深五间，重檐歇山式琉璃瓦顶。

Confucius Temple of Taikang

The temple, located on the north side of Hongxue Street in Chengguan Hui's Town, Taikang County, was an official education institution. Facing south, it was built in 1426. Lingxing Gate, and Worship and Dacheng Halls stand on the temple's central axis south to north.

扶沟大程书院

位于扶沟县城内书院街。北宋熙宁八年（1075年）至元丰三年（1080年）由程颢在扶沟任知县时所建。南北长74米，东西宽40米。大门三间，古槐一棵，龙门三间，古松两株，立雪讲堂三间，东西廊房各两排，每排13间。现存为清康熙二十八年（1689年）知县缪应缙重建。

Fugou Dacheng Academy
Located on Academy Street, Fugou County, it was built in 1075 by Cheng Hao, a Fugou County official. The existing academy, a 1689 reconstruction by an official named Miu Yingjin, is 74 meters long south to north and 40 meters wide east to west.

西华县明伦堂

位于西华县城关镇矍学街,原为学宫的一部分。始建于元代,明洪武年间(1368~1398年)重建,后世有重修。原建筑规模宏大,毁于1946年,现仅存明伦堂,面阔、进深均三间,单檐硬山小灰瓦顶。殿右侧保存明万历年间(1573~1620年)立残碑一通。

Minglun Hall, Xihua County

The hall on Hongxue Street, Chengguan Town in Xihua County, built during the Yuan Dynasty (1271-1368), was rebuilt many times. A residual stone stele from the Ming Emperor Wanli's Reign (1573-1620) is preserved beside the hall.

| 西华县城隍庙 |

位于西华县城关镇城隍庙街,始建年代不详,原建筑多毁于兵燹、洪水,明洪武三年(1370年)在原址重建,明清多次修葺、扩建。现存前殿,面阔、进深均三间,单檐硬山灰筒瓦顶,殿前有卷棚顶拜殿。

Chenghuang Temple of Xihua County

The temple at Chenghuang Temple Street, Chengguan Town, Xihua County, was rebuilt at the original site in 1370, its first construction date was unknown. Front and worship halls remain.

太康小吴塔

位于太康县逊母口镇小吴村东南,建于清乾隆年间(1736～1795年),为六角六级密檐式砖塔,通高14.8米。塔身四、五层辟佛龛,内置佛像12尊,塔顶置宝塔式塔刹。

Xiaowu Pagoda of Taikang County

The pagoda, located southeast of Xiaowu Village in Xunmukou Town, Taikang County, is more than 200 years old. The spire topped, hexagonal six-storey brick pagoda with dense eaves is 14.8 meters tall. Inside the pagoda are 12 enshrined Buddha statues.

太康寿圣寺塔

位于太康县高贤乡高贤集东街，始建于宋明道二年（1033年），明正德十三年（1518年）重修，为六角七级楼阁式砖塔，通高29米。一至六层南面辟有门，檐下施砖雕斗拱。六层共嵌石雕佛像211尊，题记铭石14方。

Shousheng Temple Pagoda in Taikang

Located on Jidong Street, Gaoxian, Taikang County, the temple was constructed in 1033 and repaired in 1518. The hexagonal, 7-storey, 29 meter tall, pavilion-style brick pagoda has 14 square meters of stone inscriptions, and is inlaid with 211 statues of the Buddha.

| 商水寿圣寺塔 |

位于商水县郝岗乡常社村西北，始建于北宋，明正统元年（1436年）重修，为六角九级楼阁式砖塔，通高42米。塔身各层辟门，塔顶置铁质宝瓶塔刹。塔内一至七层设穹隆顶塔心室，四层塔心室嵌石雕佛像三尊，七层以上塔心室为竖井式方洞，东西两壁设脚窝，可登临顶层。

Pagoda of Shousheng Temple in Shangshui

Located in northwest Changshe Village, Haogang, Shangshui County, the pagoda was built in 1033 and repaired in 1436. The hexagonal, pavilion-style, brick 9-storey pagoda is 42 meters tall. Atop it is an iron spire. Three stone Buddha statues were inlayed in the pagoda.

西华县龙泉寺

位于西华县聂堆乡思都岗村，因寺前原有古潭，泉水终年不涸而得名。始建于汉代，现存建筑为清代重修。占地一万多平方米，大殿面阔五间，进深三间，单檐硬山灰瓦顶。另存东西厢房各三间。殿前现存明、清两代重修龙泉寺碑记三通。

Longquan Temple of Xihua County

At Sidugang Village, Niedui, Xihua County, the temple was named Longquan because the spring feeding the lake in front of the temple never dries up. With a history of about 2,000 years, the existing temple and its main halls, wing rooms and stele inscriptions were repaired during the Qing Dynasty.

千年古刹支亭寺

位于扶沟县柴岗乡寺前和寺后村之间，座落在南北走向、高五米左右呈龟形状的土岗上。始建于北齐武平年间（550～581年），是在张志伯祠全神庙的旧址上修建起来。寺内设有佛祖殿、天王殿等60多间，总建筑面积2300多平方米。寺山门前的一棵千年古槐。

Zhiting Ancient Temple

Over 1,400 years old, the temple is located between Siqian and Sihou at Caigang in Fugou County. It has more than 60 buildings including Buddha and Heavenly Guardians Halls. An ancient Chinese scholar tree planted 1,000 years ago stands in front of the temple.

陈州街清真寺

　　位于周口市沙河南岸陈州街路南，建于清雍正元年（1723年）。现存大门、二门、戒墙、大拜殿、厢房、总面积3000平方米。大门、二门、厢房为硬山灰瓦顶；戒墙为砖砌四柱三楼式花墙，辟券门，并有砖砌壁龛和楹联；大拜殿面阔三间，进深三间，硬山卷棚勾连灰瓦顶，殿内悬题刻匾额。

Chenzhou Street Mosque

The Mosque is south of Chenzhou Street on the South Bank of Shahe River, Zhoukou. Built in 1723, its entrance door, second door, walls, worship halls and wing rooms are preserved. A plaque with inscriptions hangs in the main hall.

淮阳城关镇清真大寺

位于淮阳县城关镇中部,始建于唐代,明、清两代曾重建,占地近一万平方米,建大殿、卷棚、大门、南北讲堂、望月楼、女寺等。大殿彩饰华丽,遍布砖木雕作。后有损毁,1989年在原址重建,为阿拉伯式建筑风格,顶部为大型绿色装饰圆顶,上装宝瓶月牙。

Mosque of Chengguan Town Huaiyang

Located in the middle of Chengguan Town in Huaiyang County, the mosque was built during the Tang Dynasty. It consists of main hall, round ridge roof, entrance door, south and north lecture halls and Moon Watching Tower, etc. The main hall has splendid decorations and many woodcarvings.

叶氏庄园

位于商水县邓城乡邓城寨,始建于清康熙年间(1662～1722年)。四合院布局,坐北朝南,占地近两万平方米,现存一个三进院落,平房17间,楼房70间,是我国典型的硬山式四合院组群建筑。建筑飞檐斗拱,珍兽镇脊,砖木雕刻,堪称一绝。

Ye Family Manor

Ye Family Manor in Fengsheng Village of Fengsheng Town, Shangshuo County, has a 300-year history, the quadrangle courtyard-style manor faces south. A large courtyard, 17 single-storey houses and 70 buildings remain. The structure features cornices, brackets and brick and woodcarvings.

袁世凯故居

位于项城王明口乡，是袁世凯出生及童年居住地。始建于清咸丰八年（1858年），为四合院建筑，分左、中、右三处院落，原有房舍200余间，占地面积约四万平方米。现存50余间，右院西侧有花园，存假山、水池、凉亭等建筑，均硬山灰瓦顶。

Former Residence of Yuan Shikai

Located at Wangmingkou Village in Xiangcheng, it was a birthplace and former residence of Yuan Shikai, the first president of the Republic of China. The quadrangle courtyard residence was built in 1858 with more than 200 rooms; only 50 or so survive.

袁世凯行宫（项城博物馆）

位于项城市十字街西南隅，始建于清光绪三十三年（1907年）。坐西向东，有左、中、右三轴三进院落组成，原有楼瓦房99间，现存中院、后院二进院落建筑11栋，48间，均为硬山灰瓦顶。

Temporary Imperial Palace of Yuan Shikai (Xiangcheng Museum)

The palace, built in 1907 at the southwest corner of Shizi Street in Xiangcheng, faces east and used to have three courtyards and 99 tile-roofed houses; only 48 in the middle courtyard and backyard remain.

吉鸿昌将军纪念馆

　　原为扶沟县烈士陵园，1964 年建成，1984 年改为现名。新址设在县城南三环路侧，占地 6300 平方米。新的纪念馆已于 2009 年 11 月 24 日，吉鸿昌将军就义 75 周年之际开馆。

General Ji Hongchang Memorial Hall

Built in 1964, the memorial hall used to be Martyrs' Park of Fugou County; it was renamed in 1984. The new site is located beside Third Ring Road in south Fugou County. The memorial hall was open to the public 24 November 2009, the 75th anniversary of the general's sacrifice.

| 逍遥镇水闸 |

位于逍遥镇北部的颍河,建有20世纪60、70年代时期水闸,桥闸两用,上有"全世界无产阶级联合起来、团结起来争取更大的胜利、革命是历史的火车头"等标语多处。

Water Gate of Xiaoyao Town

The water gate, at Yinghe River north of Xiaoyao Town, was built in the 1960s and 1970s. It also serves as a bridge.

周口公园

　　位于周口市川汇区文昌大道与东环交汇处，是周口东新区建设的一项公益性重点工程。公园占地约50多万平方米，其中水面17多万平方米。大门为乳白色仿西洋式建筑，大门外广场中植有各种乔灌木、草坪、花卉等。

Zhoukou Park

The Park is at the junction of Wenchang Avenue and East Ring Road in Chuanhui District, Zhoukou. The water surface totals more than 170,000 square meters. The park gate is a Western-style. Various tree and shrub species, grasses, flowers and plants can be seen everywhere in the park.

周口市博物馆

位于周口市东新区文昌大道东段,占地16万多平方米。基本陈列为《宛丘之上——周口历史文物陈列》,共分为"人文肇始""大道幽微""三代华章""莽原鸿爪""逐波兴埠"五个部分,是展示周口悠久历史和灿烂文化的重要窗口。

Zhoukou City Museum

The museum is located at the east section of Wenchang Road in Dongxin District, Zhoukou. Five exhibitions at the museum show the long history and splendid culture of the Chinese nation.

西华胡辣汤

又名糊辣汤,是中国北方早餐中常见的传统汤类名吃。按宋代医书《太平惠民和剂局方》记载,在食物里加入辛温香燥药物有益行气,早在宋代辛辣味食品已经开始流行。周口西华县逍遥镇胡辣汤最为出名,由多种天然中草药按比例配制的汤料再加入胡椒、辣椒,又用骨头汤熬制而成。

Xihua Pepper Soup

Known as spicy soup, it is the common traditional soup served in breakfast in northern China. The pepper soup in Xiaoyao Town, Xihua County, Zhoukou, is the most famous. The soup is cooked with multiple natural herbs according to the proportion, which will be added in pepper, chili and bones.

| 扶沟县烟雾山庙会 |

位于扶沟县韭园镇,又名烟雾山、乌鸦山,是"中岳"嵩山山脉余支。系道教圣地,山上建有将军殿、老君殿、玉皇殿、王母殿、人祖殿、祖师殿、老母殿等仿古建筑。山后有一古刹白云寺。每逢三月三、六月初一古庙会时,香客如云、人山人海、热闹非凡。

Temple Fair of Yanwu Mountain Fugou County

Located at Jiuyuan Town in Fugou County, at Yanwu Mountain (also called Crow Mountain, section of the Mount Song Range),there are many arched main. Behind the mountain is Baiyun Temple, where temple fairs are held on the third day of lunar March and the first day of lunar June each year. Huge crowds attend every year.

周口越调

越调是河南省周口市的传统戏剧,是河南省的三大剧种之一。越调原称"四股弦",因其伴奏乐器为象鼻四弦而得名。其演出形式有皮影越调戏、木偶越调戏、越调大戏班三种。

Yue Opera of Zhoukou

The traditional opera of Zhoukou, Yue Opera is one of the three major operas in Henan Province. Named after an accompaniment of musical instrument, Yue Opera was originally, called "Four Strings", is performed in three forms: shadow puppet, puppet show and theatrical troupe.

太昊陵庙会

太昊陵，俗称人祖庙。据考，太昊伏羲陵始建于春秋，汉代曾在陵前建祠。太昊伏羲陵占地36万平方米，其规模之宏大，建筑之雄伟，世人叹绝。每年自农历二月二日始，至三月三日止，会期一个月，太昊陵庙会的声势之大、会期之长为中原地区庙会所独有。

Taihao Mausoleum Temple Fair in Huaiyang Zhoukou

Taihao Mausoleum is commonly known as Renzu Temple. Historical records show the Mausoleum is more than 2,000 years old. The temple fair starts here from the second day of lunar February and ends on the third day of lunar March with a long span of one month making it unique among temple fairs in the Central Plains.

> 官会锣鼓

是流行于项城市官会镇的民间打击乐器形式，在北宋时期就远近闻名。以铜锣为道具，时而打时而舞，并用锣组成各种造型。在官会响锣基础上改编的官会锣龙舞，把民间流传的龙舞、鬼舞与抬花轿舞巧妙运用到官会锣鼓中，曾获多个奖项，是民间艺术的瑰宝。

Guanhui Gongs and Drums

Popular folk percussion instruments of Guanhui Town in Xiangcheng, Guanhui gongs and drums have a history of nearly 1,000 years. Combining dancing with instrument playing, gongs and drums are used in all kinds of dances.

祭拜伏羲大典

淮阳，古称宛丘、陈州，是远古时期位居三皇之首的太昊伏羲氏定都和长眠之地，中华姓氏文化、农耕文化的发源地之一。每年的农历二月初二，是为期一月的统太昊陵庙会的第一天。数万群众赶来逛庙会、拜羲皇。淮阳人祖庙会、"太昊伏羲祭典"被列入"中国民族民间文化保护工程"和国家非物质文化遗产名录。

Worship Ceremony of Fu Xi in Huaiyang Zhoukou

Huaiyang is the resting place of the Chinese ancient Emperor Fu Xi and where he established his capital. Huaiyang is one of the origins of the Chinese surname culture and farming culture. The month-long Taihao Mausoleum temple fair starts on the second day of lunar February, during which thousands of people attend and worship Fu Xi.

太康道情戏

流行于太康县及周边地区，有近200年历史。源于道教乐歌，唱时配以鱼皮筒鼓伴奏，又称"鱼鼓道情"。以唱为主，剧本多唱词而少插白。据统计有30多个曲牌、曲调，包括三大类、五大品种。现存传统剧目70多部，现代剧目40多部。曲调纯厚朴实，唱词通俗易懂，深受人民群众喜爱。

Taikang Daoqing Opera (Rhyme of Taoist)

A popular opera focused on singing in Taikang County and nearby areas, Taikang Daoqing opera has a nearly 200-year history. More than 70 traditional and over 40 modern Taikang Daoqing operas have been passed down.

淮阳县泥泥狗

　　流行于淮阳县城东北的金庄、盛庄、陈楼等村庄，是一种民间泥塑艺术。泥泥狗是其中有特色的一种，其它有"草帽老虎""猴头燕尾""四不象""歪嘴斑鸠""甩尾连鱼""猴骑猫"等，造型古拙神奇。在每年农历二月二的太昊陵庙会上引人注目，泥塑被视作辟凶、纳吉求子的吉祥物。

Huaiyang County Clay Dog
This is a kind of folk clay sculpture art popular in Jinzhuang, Shengzhuang and Chenlou villages in Huaiyang County. Clay dogs are one of the many clay sculpture shapes considered to prevent bad luck and bring good luck.

周口渔鼓

又叫道情，或叫渔鼓道情、仙戏，俗称"梆梆筒子"。其形式是用三尺三寸长的竹筒，两端蒙上皮，配上木筒板拍打发出响音说唱。目前，在商水县还能唱渔鼓的艺人有商水县舒庄乡杜店村的杜三合和他的女弟子赵春。

Zhoukou Bamboo Drum

Also called Daoqing, Bamboo drum of Daoqing or Xianxi. It is commonly known as "Bang Bang Tongzi" in Chinese; it is a percussion instrument made of a one-meter lengths of bamboo used to accompany the chanting of folk tales.

沈丘回族文狮舞

最早发源于汉唐时期的西域"五方狮子舞"和"胡人假狮子"。南宋端平元年（1234年）蒙古军平定中原后，一名叫海鼻耳的波斯人，跟随蒙军征战至项城（今沈丘槐店），后在此地进行传教布道过程中，将西域的狮子舞与当地春节舞龙闹灯的风俗相结合而形成。现仍流传于当地回民生活区。

Shenqiu Hui People's Lion Dance

This dance first originated from the western region during the Han and Tang dynasties. When the Mongols conquered the Central Plains in 1234, the Persian who followed the Mongol army created the Lion Dance by combining the lion dancing style from the western region and Central Plains' Spring Festival dragon dance custom.